BrightRED Study Guide

Curriculum for Excellence

N5

HOSPITALITY: PRACTICAL CAKE CRAFT

Pam Thomas

BrightRED
PUBLISHING

First published in 2014 by:
Bright Red Publishing Ltd
1 Torphichen Street
Edinburgh
EH3 8HX

A CIP record for this book is available from the British Library

ISBN 978-1-906736-55-2

With thanks to:
PDQ Digital Media Solutions Ltd (layout), Sue Moody, Bright Writing (edit) and Ian Garioch (photography)

Cover design and series book design by Caleb Rutherford – e i d e t i c

Acknowledgements
Every effort has been made to seek all copyright holders. If any have been overlooked, then Bright Red Publishing will be delighted to make the necessary arrangements.

Permission has been sought from all relevant copyright holders and Bright Red Publishing are grateful for the use of the following:
Cover of Baking Heaven Magazine © Anthem Publishing (p 6); Cover of Cake Craft & Decoration Magazine © Anglo American Media Ltd (p 6); Logo © The British Sugarcraft Guild (p 7); Cover of 'Be-Ro Home Recipes' © Premier Foods (p 7); wmstadler/freeimages.com (p 9); Mattie Hagedorn (CC BY-SA 2.0)[1] (p 9); George Redgrave (CC BY-ND 2.0)[2] (p 9); melaniemar/freeimages.com (p 9); JFXie (CC BY 2.0)[3] (p 9); Pyrex logo © Arc International Cookware SAS (p 12); Tala logo © George East (Housewares) Ltd (p 13); jazzlah (CC BY 2.0)[3] (p 18); Jkwchui (CC BY-SA 3.0)[4] (p 22); Logo © Coeliac UK (p 23); algojo/ freeimages.com (p 25); Rufino Uribe (CC BY-SA 2.0)[1] (p 26); Stanzilla (CC BY-SA 3.0)[4] (p 26); hisks/ freeimages.com (p 26); Logo © Dr. Oetker (UK) Ltd. (p 30); Ten images by Pam Thomas (pp 32 – 33); Tristan Ferne (CC BY 2.0)[3] (p 34); S C (CC BY-ND 2.0)[2] (p 35); monokini/freeimages.com (p 38); Chris Isherwood (CC BY-SA 2.0)[1] (p 38); An Mai (CC BY-SA 2.0)[1] (p 39); katrina.alana (CC BY-ND 2.0)[2] (p 39); Two images by Acadac derived from Pratheepps/Erin Silversmith (public domain) (p 40); Pam Thomas (p 41); Twentyfour Students (CC BY-SA 2.0)[1] (p 42); jazzlah (CC BY 2.0)[3] (p 42) Ginny (CC BY-SA 2.0)[1] (p 44); Joy (CC BY 2.0)[3] (p 49); Bonne Maman logo © Andros UK Ltd (p 50); Rasbak (CC BY-SA 3.0)[4] (p 51); Roozitaa (CC BY-SA 3.0)[4](p 52); Pam Thomas (p 53); James Petts (CC BY-SA 2.0)[1] (p 63); Ben Ostrowsky (CC BY 2.0)[3] (p 64); Three images by Pam Thomas (p 70 – 71); cara fealy choate (CC BY 2.0)[3] (p 72); Eight images by Pam Thomas (pp 72 – 83); David Holt (CC BY-SA 2.0)[1] (p 85); Pam Thomas (p 85); Henrycooksey (CC BY 3.0)[5] (p 86); Mikelo (CC BY-SA 2.0)[1] (p 87); Mattie Hagedorn (CC BY-SA 2.0)[1] (p 87); Two images by Pam Thomas (pp 87 – 88); Alan Clark (CC BY 2.0)[3] (p 88); Matthew Bietz (CC BY-SA 2.0)[1] (p 89); The Integer Club (CC BY 2.0)[3] (p 90); Gordon Joly (CC BY-SA 2.0)[1] (p 91); Ayca Wilson (CC BY 2.0)[3] (p 91); geryy/freeimages.com (p 92); Alpha (CC BY-SA 2.0)[1] (p 92); Douglas Paul Perkins (CC BY 3.0)[5] (p 92); bongo vongo (CC BY-SA 2.0)[1] (p 93); David Holt (CC BY-SA 2.0)[1] (p 94); Alpha (CC BY-SA 2.0)[1] (p 93); Kelly Hunter (CC BY 2.0)[3] (p 95).

(CC BY-SA 2.0)[1] http://creativecommons.org/licenses/by-sa/2.0/
(CC BY-ND 2.0)[2] http://creativecommons.org/licenses/by-nd/2.0/
(CC BY 2.0)[3] http://creativecommons.org/licenses/by/2.0/
(CC BY-SA 3.0)[4] http://creativecommons.org/licenses/by-sa/3.0/
(CC BY 3.0)[5] http://creativecommons.org/licenses/by/3.0/

Printed and bound in the UK.

CONTENTS LIST

INTRODUCING NATIONAL 5 PRACTICAL CAKE CRAFT

Hospitality: Practical Cake Craft sits within the Social Studies curriculum area of the Curriculum for Excellence.

The course focuses on the development of practical, technical and creative skills in cake baking and cake finishing. It will enable you to develop an understanding of the scientific nature of cake production, how to adapt basic recipes and create new flavour combinations, as well as develop and demonstrate highly imaginative techniques in the design and production of a range of cakes and other baked items.

It is a predominantly practical course that links to the growth industry of artisan bakery and confectionary. During the course, you will develop a range of artistic techniques and, drawing on all aspects of design such as shape, colour, texture, balance and precision, you will be given the opportunity to create and produce a variety of individualised products and to creatively interpret a design brief.

This book focuses on the core content of the National 5 syllabus for Practical Cake Craft. There are two mandatory units: Cake Baking and Cake Finishing. In addition, there is a section on the course assessment which must be passed to gain the course award.

EXTERNAL ASSESSMENT

At the end of the course, you will be assessed externally by one component:

- Component 1 – Practical Activity – 100 % of total mark

The purpose of the course assessment is to assess added value. The practical activity draws on the knowledge, understanding and skills developed across the course. The assessment requires you to demonstrate your knowledge and understanding of cake baking, finishing and evaluating in response to a given design brief.

PRACTICAL ACTIVITY

The purpose of the practical activity is to assess your ability to apply the skills required to bake and finish a cake to a given design brief.

It has three stages:

- Designing   10 marks (includes producing a design illustration and a plan of work).
- Implementing 85 marks (includes baking and finishing the cake according to the plan).
- Evaluating   5 marks (includes reflection on the quality of the finished result).

A cake design brief will be provided by SQA.

The practical activity will be carried out under supervised conditions to ensure that the work presented is your own work, and will be quality assured by SQA (Scottish Qualifications Authority).

INTERNAL ASSESSMENT

During the course, you will be assessed on a wide range of skills, including the ability to:

- bake a range of different cakes and baked products
- use specialist tools and equipment with dexterity and flair
- creatively apply finishing techniques to cakes and other baked items
- demonstrate creativity and resourcefulness in the overall presentation of the finished cake
- demonstrate effective organisation and time management skills
- interpret and carry out a practical activity to meet the requirements of a design brief
- work safely and hygienically
- evaluate both the product and the process.

COURSE CONTENT

The course has two mandatory units: Cake Baking and Cake Finishing.

CAKE BAKING

The aim of this unit is to enable you to develop the ability to bake a range of cakes and other items safely and hygienically, while demonstrating specialist skills, techniques and processes. You will also learn about the value of accurate weighing and measuring, the function of different ingredients and how to combine these using different methods of cake production.

This unit will develop your ability to prepare equipment and ingredients effectively and efficiently, which in turn will help your final product to be successful.

To promote personalisation and choice, this unit provides opportunities to investigate baking trends and allows you to apply this knowledge in a range of practical contexts.

CAKE FINISHING

The aim of this unit is to develop your ability to finish a range of cakes and other baked items safely and hygienically. During the finishing processes, you will produce and apply a range of different coatings and fillings, plus apply specialised skills and creative techniques including piping, modelling, stencilling, crimping and embossing. To promote personalisation and choice, this unit allows opportunities to investigate trends in cake finishing and allows you to apply this knowledge in a range of practical contexts.

This book has been developed using an interactive, contemporary approach which acknowledges the fast-paced technological society we live in. Its broad range of activities and visual appeal have been devised to offer you lots of choice, enabling you to engage with a range of abilities and learning styles. It is also an effective tool for independent study.

ONLINE

This book is supported by the Bright Red Digital Zone. Visit www.brightedbooks. net/N5PCC and register to unlock extra content, tests, videos and more.

PREPARING FOR BAKING: SELECTING RECIPES

FINDING THE RIGHT RECIPE

A great cake begins with the right recipe. However, as any baker can tell you, finding the right recipe is easier said than done. There are thousands of cake recipe books, many of them promising 'easy' recipes that will yield delicious cakes. There are plenty of online resources to help you sift through the mountains of cake recipes at your disposal, such as www.allrecipes.com where thousands of users submit and rate cake recipes.

You can also go on to an internet discussion board to discuss issues with other bakers and get suggestions for recipes. So how do you choose? Let's look at possible sources of great recipes!

INTERNET

The internet provides a wealth of resources, where you can find a huge range of recipes for any baked goods you want to make. A word of warning however, you might find yourself on an American site where the measurements are in cups instead of grams, or the recipe includes ingredients you might not be able to source or be in large quantities that you need to scale down. Stick to tried-and-tested websites. Sites that have reviews or feedback from those who have tried the recipe are always useful.

Why not try the following:

- www.bbc.co.uk/food
- www.deliaonline.com
- www.maryberry.co.uk/recipes
- www.bakingmad.com

Internet blogs include: http://junipercakery.co.uk/blog/, http://www.thepinkwhisk.co.uk/, http://www.magentacakes.co.uk/blog/, http://www.bbc.co.uk/blogs/food/2012/08/cake-man-v-machine.shtml. To find other useful baking blogs, just use a search engine and type in 'cake recipes' or 'cake baking blogs'.

MAGAZINES

There are a wide range of specialist magazines that cover cake baking and decorating. You might be able to access some of these via your local library. Some also have online websites. Magazines are a great way to keep up with baking trends, plus they usually offer good seasonal ideas for baked items for you to try. Some popular magazines include *Baking Heaven*, *Delicious*, *Cake Craft & Decoration*, *Cake Decorating* and *BBC Good Food*.

TV PROGRAMMES

Baking is very topical at the moment and there are lots of programmes on television that you could watch to find out more about, or enhance your skills in, both baking and decorating. Again, a word of warning here: recipe quantities might be given quickly by the presenter, so it's always a good idea to be prepared with pen/paper as you watch. If you miss the programme, there is always the option of using catch-up services. Some popular programmes might also be released onto DVD.

Some shows worth considering include:

- *The Home of Fabulous Cakes*
- *Ace of Cakes*
- *Lorraine Pascale's Kitchen*
- *The Great British Bake Off*
- *Bake with Anna Olson*
- The Good Food Channel
- *The Fabulous Baker Brothers* via Channel 4 Food

ONLINE

Check out the links to the homepages of great baking shows at www.brightredbooks.net/N5PCC

SHOWS AND COMPETITIONS

Attending shows, such as Cake International (http://www.cakeinternational.co.uk/) and The Cake and Bake Show (http://thecakeandbakeshow.co.uk/manchester/), will give you an ideal opportunity to attend tutorials, demonstrations and see fantastic examples of cakes that have been entered into the various competitions. However, as a starting point, why not look at what's on offer closer to home – is there a village show that you can enter your cakes into?

THE BRITISH SUGARCRAFT GUILD

The British Sugarcraft Guild came into being in 1981. It aims to 'promote and stimulate interest in sugarcraft, share knowledge, develop talent and improve standards'. There are over 100 local branches throughout the country. Their website can be found at www.bsguk.org. Branches in Scotland all come under **Region 1**. It has its own website: http://bsgregion1.webs.com/. If you are aged up to 18, you can join the Guild as a 'cygnet' for a small fee. By doing so, you are eligible to enter BSG competitions, or you can just go along to Guild meetings and learn from the experienced members who attend.

ONLINE

Visit www.brightredbooks.net/N5PCC and follow the link to 'The British Sugarcraft Guild' for more information.

ONLINE

Follow the 'Be-Ro' link at www.brightredbooks.net/N5PCC

BOOKS

There are many cookery books on the market that provide a wealth of recipes to try. Use trial and error to find out which ones are successful. One small recipe book that has stood the test of time is the Be-Ro book. It has been on the go since the 1920s and is still an invaluable bakery book to use today.

Well-known bakers including Delia Smith and Mary Berry have cake baking and decorating books that you could check out for suitable recipes.

There are also tried-and-tested recipes within this book (see pages 86–95).

ONLINE

When looking at a recipe, you need to take into account the quantities of ingredients and the size of the tin. If you need to scale your recipe, but get stuck with the maths, you could try the app called 'The CakeOmeter': just put in your quantities and size of tin and it'll do all the work for you! Find the link at www.brightredbooks.net/N5PCC

THINGS TO DO AND THINK ABOUT

Head off to your local library to see what they have in the way of books, magazines and DVDs all about cake baking and decorating.

ONLINE TEST

How well have you learned this topic? Take the 'Selecting recipes' test at www.brightredbooks.net/N5PCC

PLANNING THE STAGES OF BAKING

You will be assessed on your ability to plan the stages of baking as part of the Cake Baking unit. Your plans should include all the key tasks for preparation and baking in a logical order. How you design your plan is up to you.

WRITING A PLAN

You may want to write down a **numbered list**, like a recipe method – for example:

1 Wash hands, put apron on.

2 Grease and prepare the tin.

3 Pre-heat the oven to 180°C.

4 Collect ingredients.

5 Accurately weigh and measure them out.

6 Add the margarine and sugar into a large bowl, and cream.

You could consider adding in a section at the beginning that includes equipment you need to gather together before you start working. This could really help you to get organised and it will save you time and allow you to focus totally on the activity you are undertaking.

Another useful tip is to have a column where you can add notes or write down points as you work through the activity. These notes could really help you the next time you complete a similar task.

You may want to add a bit more detail and complete your planning in the form of a **time plan**:

EXAMPLE

9.00–9.05 Wash hands, put apron on.

9.05–9.10 Grease and prepare the tin.

9.10–9.20 Pre-heat the oven to 180°C. Collect ingredients. Accurately weigh and measure them out.

9.20–9.25 Add the margarine and sugar into a large bowl and cream together.

If you opt for this method, remember to use short, focused statements in your time plan and do **not** re-write your recipe. You could use a highlighter pen to pick out the really important points.

Don't forget to add reminders relating to hygiene and safety and if you are putting something into the oven, it is a good idea to note the time when you need to check it and remove it from the oven!

You could choose to complete a **flow chart**:

EXAMPLE

Wash hands, put on apron.

↓

Grease and prepare the tin.

↓

Pre-heat the oven to 180°C. Collect ingredients. Weigh and measure them out.

↓

Cream the margarine and sugar together in a large bowl.

contd

If you don't want to or can't write down your planning stages, then you could film yourself talking through them or you could produce a **pictorial plan**:

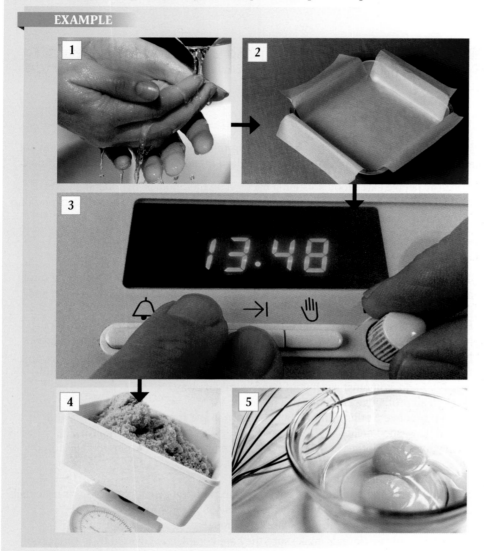

EXAMPLE

It is a good idea when undertaking the planning to think about the checks you will need to make to ensure your cake mixture is the correct consistency. You could also include a note to yourself to check that you have added all the required ingredients. It's your plan – it should be a working document that helps you bake a successful cake.

THINGS TO DO AND THINK ABOUT

Think about how to organise and store the recipes that are most successful and that you would want to bake again. You could personalise a folder, and create a recipe index with space to write your comments. These can help you the next time you make these recipes.

ONLINE TEST

How well have you learned this topic? Take the 'Planning the stages of baking' test at www.brightredbooks.net/N5PCC

ONLINE

The link at www.brightredbooks.net/N5PCC will show you one example of a short video clip that takes you very clearly through the stages of making a biscuit. Why not produce your own filmed plan of work?

HYGIENE AND SAFETY

It is essential that you maintain a satisfactory standard of personal and kitchen hygiene and safety when carrying out practical activities.

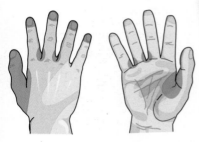

■ Areas most frequently missed during hand washing
■ Less frequently missed

□ Not missed

Bacteria on hands

ONLINE

Revision notes on this topic are available by following the 'Hygiene Fact File' link at www.brightredbooks.net/N5PCC

VIDEO LINK

Watch the video at www.brightredbooks.net/N5PCC to find out more about the importance of hand washing in food hygiene.

PERSONAL HYGIENE

Personal hygiene relates to the person handling the food. An important way to prevent food contamination is to maintain a high standard of personal hygiene and cleanliness.

Even healthy people carry food poisoning bacteria on their bodies. By touching parts of your body, such as your nose, mouth, hair (where you find a bacterium called *Staphylococcus aureus*), or your clothes you can spread bacteria from your hands to the food.

Prevent the spread of bacteria that can lead to food poisoning by practising good personal hygiene:

- Thoroughly wash and dry your hands with soap and hot water before handling food, after using the toilet and after you have blown your nose. Don't forget to wash and dry them again frequently during food preparation.
- Dry your hands with clean towels, disposable paper towels or under an air dryer.
- Never smoke, chew gum, spit, or eat/drink in a food handling or food storage area.
- Never cough or sneeze over food or where food is prepared or stored.
- Fingers should not be licked. Care should be taken not to touch your nose/mouth/hair. If you do, you must wash your hands straight away.
- Wear clean protective clothing such as an apron.
- Clean protective clothing should only be worn in the food preparation area and should be washed daily.
- Keep your spare clothes and other personal items away from where food is stored and prepared.
- If you have long hair, tie it back or cover it.
- Keep your nails short so they are easy to clean, and don't wear nail polish or false nails as varnish can chip into the food or false nails could come loose.
- Avoid wearing jewellery, or only wear plain banded rings and sleeper earrings.
- If you have cuts or wounds, make sure they are completely covered by a waterproof wound strip or a bandage. Use brightly coloured (blue) wound strips, so they can be seen easily if they fall off.
- Wear disposable gloves over the top of the wound strip if you have wounds on your hands.
- Change disposable gloves regularly.
- Advise your supervisor if you feel unwell and don't handle food. If you have a problem that relates to your nose, skin, throat, stomach, or if you have bowel trouble or an infected wound, it is a legal requirement that you inform your supervisor.

DON'T FORGET

If you don't clean your work surface properly after cutting cake, you will get crumbs in your icing, which will definitely not give your cake a professional finish!

KITCHEN HYGIENE

- Check work surfaces and equipment to make sure they are clean before you start to prepare food, and clean them thoroughly afterwards.
- Adopt a 'clean-as-you-go' approach to working.
- Wipe up any spills immediately. This is not only good practice in relation to preventing bacterial growth, but it also prevents the chance of anyone slipping and falling.
- Make sure food is covered at all times to prevent contamination with bacteria.
- Store all perishable food in a refrigerator. This should be checked regularly to ensure it is working at 0–5°C.
- Use disposable cloths for cleaning and never dry hands on a cloth designed to dry dishes.
- Dispose of all waste into a bin with a lid.

contd

- Avoid damaging the work surface with a sharp knife – where possible, always cut on a protective board, as bacteria can harbour in these areas.

SAFETY

- Never place a sharp knife into a basin of water and forget about it. Wash it straight away, dry carefully and put it back into a knife block, making sure that you transport it with the blade down by your side when moving around the room.
- Never handle electrical equipment with wet hands.
- Don't run in the kitchen at any time.
- If you are uncertain about what size of saucepan to use, then consider using a slightly larger one, as the contents will be less likely to boil over. Make sure the pan is on the correct size of ring and that the handle is over to the side of the cooker to avoid it being knocked over.
- Always use oven gloves when taking a hot tray or cake tin out of the oven, and place onto a wooden pot stand or heatproof mat to protect the work surface.

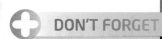

DON'T FORGET

If you don't clean piping nozzles straight after you use them, they can become clogged with hardened icing and might have to be replaced. Also, unclean crimpers or plunge cutters can transfer unwanted leftover colour if not washed properly after use.

Cleaning a piping nozzle.

FOOD SAFETY

ADDITIVES

If you are going to use food colouring to colour sugarpaste, it's important that you know that many of the popular colours have legal restrictions limiting the amount that can be present in a finished product. Don't panic – it will probably never be a problem unless you plan to cover a whole cake in a very dark icing to sell to a customer. However, rules on the use of food **additives** are extremely important to the food industry. The limit for many colourings is **0.5 g of E number colour per 1 kg of icing.** Common colours worth watching out for include: E102 Tartrazine, E110 Sunset Yellow, E120 Cochineal and E151 Brilliant Black.

FRESH FLOWERS

Fresh flowers on a cake can be popular – especially on wedding cakes. However, **no part of a** fresh flower is allowed to come into contact with a cake. Flowers should be arranged on a board to ensure they don't touch the surface of the cake.

WIRES AND PINS

Inserting any solid object into a cake could lead to physical contamination, which could result in injury to health. **Never** insert a pin or wire directly into a cake. Double sided sticky tape can be used to secure ribbon to the cake and a **posy pick** can be used if you plan to decorate a cake using anything on a wire.

COLD PORCELAIN

Cold porcelain is a popular medium for making flowers and decorations for cakes, as it produces long-lasting results. However, it contains glue so it must not be placed directly on a cake. As with fresh flowers, always make sure a board is used to separate the decoration from the surface of the cake.

NUTS

Nuts – peanuts in particular – are one of the most common allergy-causing foods and can cause a severe reaction called anaphylaxis in sufferers. It's always worth remembering that even if you don't include nuts in your cake, they could be present in other ingredients or they could have been be used to make something else in the kitchen. There could, therefore, be a risk of contamination. The key thing is to check with the person eating the cake and advise them that you cannot guarantee it is nut free.

THINGS TO DO AND THINK ABOUT

Design a display for the classroom that highlights the importance of caring for your cake decorating equipment.

ONLINE TEST

How well have you learned this topic? Take the 'Hygiene and safety' test at www.brightredbooks.net/N5PCC

WEIGHING AND MEASURING

THE IMPORTANCE OF ACCURACY

Baking a cake isn't quite the same as making a pot of soup. A chef can pretty much add what they want to the soup and still be able to adjust the flavour and consistency; however, a baker needs to follow the quantities noted on a recipe with a high degree of accuracy if the end product is to be a success. Remember, most bakery items are actually made out of the same ingredients – fat, flour, sugar and eggs – with only the method of preparation or quantities/proportion of ingredients varying.

WEIGHING SCALES

Traditionally, balance scales were used in baking. However, most bakers now use digital electronic scales.

To make sure your scales give you the accuracy you need, you must do the following:

- Always keep them clean and free from particles of food.
- Place the scales on a flat, secure surface to avoid any vibrations, as this may cause the reading to change.
- Do not place (or store) the scales near a microwave as the electromagnetic waves they give out can not only affect the reading but can drain the batteries.
- If the food to be weighed is very hot or very cold, place a plate on the weighing scale to insulate the scales and prevent the reading being inaccurate.
- Always make sure the display is at ZERO before starting to weigh out any ingredients.
- Some scales offer the option of weighing out in grams (g), ounces (oz), millilitres (ml) or fluid ounces (fl oz) – remember to make sure you choose the correct option for the food you are weighing.

DON'T FORGET

1000 g = 1 kg

DON'T FORGET

16 oz = 1 lb

DON'T FORGET

1000 ml = 1 l

DON'T FORGET

1 pint = 568 ml

UNITS OF MEASUREMENT

Most recipes will show ingredient weights in grams (g) or kilograms (kg).

Some might be in ounces (oz) or pounds (lb).

1 oz = 28.35 g

Some recipes – especially American ones – give ingredient weights in 'cups'.

¼ cup flour = approx 35 g

¼ cup caster sugar = approx 50 g

⅓ cup flour = approx 50 g

⅓ cup caster sugar = approx 70 g

½ cup flour = approx 75 g

½ cup caster sugar = approx 110 g

1 cup flour = approx 150 g

1 cup caster sugar = approx 220 g

contd

VOLUME MEASUREMENTS

Whereas weight is measured in grams, volume is measured in millilitres and litres.

You might also see a recipe asking for a ½ pint or a pint of liquid.

Ideally, you would want to use a measuring jug that would give you measurements for both pints and millilitres. It's important that you place the measuring jug on a level surface and check the measure at eye level to ensure accuracy.

If you only have electronic weighing scales, consider the following:

1 ml of water weighs 1 gram, so a recipe calling for 300 ml of water (or milk) can simply be substituted with 300 g of water/milk.

1 fluid ounce of water weighs approximately 1 ounce, so a recipe calling for a UK pint (20 fl oz) of water can be substituted with 20 oz of water.

HANDY MEASURES

In the absence of weighing scales, you can use the following handy measures. Note, however, that these won't guarantee you the same accuracy as scales, because you have to take the type of ingredient that you are weighing into account, along with its density.

A 'measuring cone' is a conical-shaped jug that is used to measure dry ingredients. It features a variety of different scales (depending on the ingredient that you are measuring) that can easily be seen from the inside of the jug. However, a word of warning: it might not be quite as accurate as using electronic scales.

THINGS TO DO AND THINK ABOUT

1 Make up your own 'cup-to-grams' handy reference guide. First, select a tea cup that you could use on a regular basis when baking. You will need electronic weighing scales, some ingredients (flour, sugar, water) and a pen. Fill in the following table with your results.

Ingredient	Cup	Grams (g)	Ingredient	Cup	Grams (g)

2 Why not try this simple **Fruit Bran Loaf** recipe to try out your cup measurements:

INGREDIENTS
1 cup All-Bran
1 cup dried mixed fruit
1 ½ cups milk
1 cup self-raising flour
½ cup soft brown sugar
METHOD
1. Preheat oven to 180°C/Gas 4. Grease and line a loaf tin.
2. Combine All-Bran, milk, sugar and mixed fruit in a bowl. Leave to stand for 15 mins.
3. Add the flour and mix well to combine. Spoon into the prepared tin.
4. Bake for 40 mins, or until skewer inserted comes out clear.
5. Allow to cool in tin before turning out onto wire rack.

BEWARE

Word of warning: If your recipe asks you to weigh out water or milk, you will get an accurate measurement using either weighing scales or a measuring jug. However, not all liquids can be treated the same. Some ingredients like syrup or treacle have a greater **density**. This means the particles that make up the ingredient are closely packed together, so it will weigh more.

TOP TIP

By placing your tin of syrup or treacle into a pan of boiling water for a few minutes you make the syrup/treacle flow more easily. This is known as its **viscosity**. It is much easier to measure out when it flows better. On cooling, it returns to its original viscose state.

DON'T FORGET

If your recipe asks for half an egg, first crack and beat the whole egg in a cup, then measure out half into a similar sized cup. For a large egg, this will be around 25 ml.

DON'T FORGET

1 teaspoon (tsp) = 5 ml
1 dessert spoon (dsp) = 10 ml
1 tablespoon (tbsp) = 15 ml
= 25 g

ONLINE TEST

How well have you learned this topic? Take the 'Weighing and measuring' test at www.brightredbooks.net/N5PCC

ONLINE

There are lots of different weight conversion sites you can use that will make it easy for you to adapt your recipe if you need to. Follow the link at www.brightredbooks.net/N5PCC for a good example!

CATEGORIES OF BAKED ITEMS AND BASIC RECIPES 1

A SLICE OF CAKE HISTORY

The first cakes were very similar to bread. The Romans sometimes added egg or butter, sweetened the dough with honey and included nuts or dried fruit. Although sponge cake is mentioned back in 1615, it wasn't until the eighteenth century that whisking eggs became a popular method of adding air into a cake mixture. While yeast was initially the prime raising agent, it was in the middle of the nineteenth century that a discovery was made that changed how cakes were made, how they looked and how they tasted. Alfred Bird, a British chemist, introduced an improved type of baking powder – a mixture of bicarbonate of soda and an acid – as a raising agent to be used in the place of yeast, and this really improved the end results of the cakes baked.

Four basic methods of cake making came into prominence from the mid-nineteenth century onwards:

1 Creaming method
2 Rubbing in method
3 Melted method
4 Whisking method

CREAMING METHOD

The creaming method involves creaming or beating together the fat and sugar. Using a wooden spoon, first beat the fat (which should be at room temperature) until it is soft. Add the sugar and continue to use the side of the bowl and back of the wooden spoon to cut the sugar into the fat. Doing so traps air bubbles. The mixture should look 'light and fluffy'. More air bubbles are added with the addition of beaten eggs. Flour is then gently folded in with a metal spoon, thereby avoiding knocking out any of the added air. The baking powder (either in the self-raising flour or added as a separate ingredient) begins to release carbon dioxide as soon as it enters the mixture. A little extra water (15 ml spoon) can be added at the end to soften the mixture, if required. You know you have the correct consistency when it drops off the spoon.

Once in the oven, further CO_2 is emitted so that the mixture rises to create a soft, spongy cake with a golden top, owing to the caramelisation of proteins.

The Victoria Sandwich cake is a good example of a medium sponge produced by the creaming method. It is actually not a true sponge cake, because the eggs are not whisked and fat is used; no fat is included in a true sponge. It is most closely related to the Pound Cake, an eighteenth century recipe which uses equal quantities of flour, butter, sugar and eggs in weight.

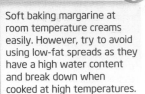

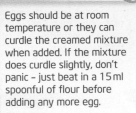

RUBBING IN METHOD

The rubbing in method consists of rubbing cold fat (ideally unsalted butter) into flour with the movement of the fingertips. The rubbing in coats the fat particles in the flour mixture so that the proteins in the flour do not form gluten links when the liquid is added. Gluten linkage is what gives bread its 'tougher' texture, as opposed to cake, which should have a lighter texture.

Cool hands are key to successful rubbing in. In addition, you should handle the fat as little as possible to prevent it melting. Rubbing in should be stopped when the mixture resembles fine breadcrumbs. The following ingredients are mixed in once the fat and flour are rubbed in and are all brought together:

- sugar
- eggs
- liquids (such as liqueurs, juices, milk)
- flavourings (such as vanilla extract or seeds, citrus peel, nuts, candied peel)
- spices (such as nutmeg, coriander, five spice, ginger, cloves or cardamom)
- fruit (such as raisins, sultanas, cranberries, dates)

Rubbing in can be done in a food processor as well as by hand.

This method is most often used for making scones, shortbread, cookies and loaf cakes.

 **DON'T FORGET**

Do not overwork the rubbed-in mixture as this will make it very difficult to work with, and will also give a poor end result.

 VIDEO LINK

The clips at www.brightredbooks.net/N5PCC will show you how to rub in correctly.

 ONLINE TEST

How well have you learned this topic? Take the 'Categories of baked items and basic recipes 1' test at www.brightredbooks.net/N5PCC

 ## THINGS TO DO AND THINK ABOUT

Why not try making a traditional Pound Cake? You can find the recipe for this on page 92.

CATEGORIES OF BAKED ITEMS AND BASIC RECIPES 2

MELTING METHOD

In the melting method, the fat, sugar and any liquid (for example, syrup, honey and treacle) are melted together before the eggs, flour and any dry ingredients are added. It is important to use a good-sized saucepan to give plenty of room to mix the ingredients. Also, stir the mixture on the hob to ensure the sugar has melted. It's important to keep the heat low so that the mixture does not bubble and burn. Make sure the mixture is allowed to cool slightly before the egg is added, as you don't want to scramble it!

Flapjacks, gingerbread and Parkin are good examples of cakes made using the melting method. Originally from the North of England, gingerbread cakes were made by mixing and baking melted butter or lard, sugar or molasses, oatmeal and ginger on the hearth or griddle. These cakes could be either thin or thick and were commonly served on Bonfire Night.

WHISKING METHOD

The whisking method produces light sponge cakes. Examples include: Genoise sponges, madeleines and Swiss roll, all of which are very soft, spongy, fluffy, light and pale.

In the whisking method, the eggs should be at room temperature. They are combined with sugar and whisked vigorously, distributing tiny air bubbles to be held in the flour mixture, which then expand in the oven. The eggs and sugar mixture can be beaten over a **bain-marie**. This allows the egg and sugar mixture to warm slightly, giving a better volume. This heat allows the protein in the egg to stretch, therefore, incorporating more air.

Baine-marie

The mixture is said to have trapped its maximum amount of air when '**ribbon trail**' stage is reached. This means that any mixture you drop from a spoon onto the mixture in the bowl will stay on top of that mixture, and won't sink into it. (See photographs to the right.) Only once you reach this stage do you start to gently fold in the flour. This can be done by using a metal spoon and a figure-of-eight type cutting method, or by using a balloon whisk. Either way, it must be done gently because if air is lost, the cake will not rise.

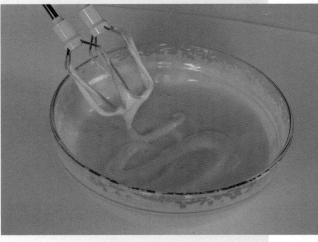
Ribbon trail

DON'T FORGET

The texture of cakes using the melting method tends to be heavier than other cakes and they won't rise as much. However, bicarbonate of soda can be used to create a lighter texture.

DON'T FORGET

You must reach ribbon trail stage in a whisked sponge before you add in any flour – doing so earlier will result in a flat cake. When you add in the flour, make sure that you fold it in gently so as not to lose any trapped air. If you whisk it, the result will again be a flat cake.

DON'T FORGET

It's always a good idea to use a glass or metal bowl when using the whisking method, as plastic bowls can often retain grease, which may affect how well the cake rises.

VIDEO LINK

Why not have a look at the clip on whisking at www.brightredbooks.net/N5PCC

CAKE CATEGORIES

To pass the Cake Baking unit, you will be required to select, plan, prepare and bake a range of cakes. At least **one** item from each of the following categories of cakes must be produced:

1 Light/medium sponge-type cakes

2 Madeira-type cakes

3 Lightly fruited cakes

4 Heavily fruited cakes

5 Traybakes/biscuits

The term 'cupcake' first appeared in the USA in the early nineteenth century. At that time, baking trays hadn't yet been invented or produced, so cakes were baked in small pottery cups – hence the name. In the 'cupcake' mixture, ingredients are measured by cup volume – that is, one cup butter, two cups sugar, three cups flour and four eggs – similar to a Pound Cake. The amount of mixture you put into the tins determines the shape of the cupcakes: half full gives a flat top, two-thirds full gives a slightly domed top and three quarters full gives a cake that has risen above the paper case and may have a crack on top.

DON'T FORGET

'Rich' cakes contain at least half the weight of fat-to-flour. The amount of fruit does not determine whether a cake is classified as rich or not.

THINGS TO DO AND THINK ABOUT

1 Check out the list of possible recipe ideas on pages 86–95 of this book. Select at least one recipe from each of the five categories. Plan and prepare the ingredients for each recipe and then bake it using safe and hygienic working practices.

ONLINE TEST

How well have you learned this topic? Take the 'Categories of baked items and basic recipes 2' test at www.brightredbooks.net/N5PCC

Category of cake	Example of type of cake	Recipe page no
Light sponge cake	Black Forest Gateau Sponge Drops Swiss Roll	87 93 94
Medium sponge cake	Carrot Cubes Pound Cake Victoria Sandwich	87 92 95
Madeira cake	Battenburg Cake Madeira Cake Marbled Chocolate and Orange Loaf	86 91 92
Lightly fruited cake	Cherry Cake Easy Fruit Slice Eggless Fruit Cake Mincemeat Tea Loaf Sultana Cake	87 89 89 92 94
Heavily fruited cake	Dundee Cake Rich Fruit Cake	88 93
Traybake	Coconut Mallow Jam Squares Ginger and Treacle Spiced Traybake Iced Lime Traybake Lemon Drizzle Cake	88 90 90 91
Biscuit	Custard Creams Empire Biscuits Viennese Fingers	88 89 95

2 You have been asked to help with the catering for a parents' evening at your school. Choose a suitable recipe for a biscuit and a traybake that can be made and served at this event.

CHEMISTRY OF COOKING

THE IMPORTANCE OF TEMPERATURE

You can do everything perfectly – select the correct ingredients, carefully weigh and measure, and prepare and deposit your cake into the tin – but if the baking temperature isn't controlled correctly then there is still a chance that your cake might fail. Many ingredients change their properties with temperature: think about what happens when fat melts, or when you add egg to a hot melted gingerbread mixture – if it's too hot, the egg cooks straight away.

Sunken cake

HEAT TRANSFER

Heat is transferred from its source to food in three main ways: conduction, convection and radiation.

CONDUCTION

Conduction is when heat passes from one hot area of an object to another. As the molecules in the food absorb heat, they vibrate and pass heat along to the next molecule and so on. Direct contact is needed for heat transfer by conduction – for example, cooking a pancake on a hot griddle.

Some baked goods are baked in a 'water bath' – for example, cheesecake. Water is slow to conduct heat so using a water bath helps the cheesecake to bake slowly and evenly.

It's worth remembering that heat conduction can be fast or slow depending upon the material that the cake tin or baking tray is made of, and how thick it is. For example, a sturdy, heavy cake tin will conduct heat more slowly, but it is often more effective because it transfers heat more evenly.

Aluminium is a good conductor of heat, and is low in cost, so it is often used to make baking trays and cake tins. However, a word of warning: it's easy to burn cakes baked in aluminium cake tins, so it's a good idea to line them with greaseproof paper.

Silicone is not a good conductor of heat. Because of this, cakes bake more slowly and brown more evenly. Silicone products are non-stick and have the ability to be used in both the oven and freezer so are extremely versatile. Just watch out when removing a silicone tin from the oven – because it's flexible and 'bendy', it's a good idea to keep it stable by putting it on a baking tray.

CONVECTION

Convection is all about heat transfer through liquids and gases. It works because warmer liquids and gases are less dense and therefore rise, while colder liquids and gases are more dense and therefore sink. This results in a constant movement – that is, a convection current. In an oven, the hot air rises to the top, but with a fan-assisted oven the hot air is forced to circulate, which should mean more even cooking in all shelves of the oven.

If you are using a fan oven, it's important to remember that they often cook 10–20° hotter than conventional ovens, so take this into account when setting the temperature. Pre-heating the oven is vital when baking cakes as the oven needs to be at the correct temperature so it can start cooking straight away. Pre-heating can take between five and 15 minutes, depending upon the temperature to be reached.

contd

VIDEO LINK

Watch the clip at www. brightredbooks.net/N5PCC to find out more about cooking in a water bath or bain-marie.

DON'T FORGET

Even when the pan is removed from the heat source, conduction continues, so the food will continue to cook.

DON'T FORGET

It's important not to overload an oven as there needs to be space between the baking trays for hot air to circulate and cook the baked goods evenly.

DON'T FORGET

Never open the oven door before the cake is ready because cool air will rush in and may cause the cake to sink.

Use the following conversion guide if your recipe doesn't give you the oven temperature for the oven you're using:

°C (CELSIUS)	°F (FAHRENHEIT)	GAS MARK
140°C	275°F	1
150°C	300°F	2
160°C	325°F	3
170°C	335°F	3/4
180°C	350°F	4
190°C	375°F	5
200°C	400°F	6
210°C	410°F	6/7
220°C	425°F	7
230°C	450°F	8
240°C	475°F	9

TOP TIP

If you are baking a batch of cookies and you need to divide them between two or more baking trays, try to put the same number of cookies on each tray so that they cook at the same rate. Ideally, switch the trays around half way through the cooking time. If you need to cook a second batch straight away, **do not** put the raw cookie dough onto the hot tray – let it cool down first. A hot baking tray might make the raw cookies spread, which will result in thin, irregular-sized cookies.

RADIATION

Radiation is the rapid transfer of heat through space from a warm heat source to the surface of a cooler one. Once the molecules on the surface of the food absorb the heat rays, they vibrate rapidly, which generates more heat within the object. In radiation, the food doesn't usually come into contact with the heat source – for example, as when bread is grilled. In an oven, heat is radiated off hot oven walls, creating hot spots along the oven walls. To prevent uneven baking, it's a good idea to place tins/trays in the centre of the oven away from the walls. In a gas oven, it's really important not to place the tray too close to the flame at the back.

Radiation is also the way heat is transferred in a microwave. When microwaving food, heat is generated when the food particles heat up and the molecules move about frantically. Heating with microwaves is fast because the radiant waves penetrate into the centre of the food. Just remember that you need to use microwave-safe containers to bake cakes – silicone is fine. To ensure that you get a successful outcome, it's a good idea to cook on 80 per cent of full power. Remember that the cake will still be cooking after it comes out of the oven. A standard microwave will not brown the top of the cake, so chocolate cakes are usually more successful than other types of sponges made in microwaves.

THINGS TO DO AND THINK ABOUT

1   If you are going to be using the same oven for a regular period, it's a good idea to know whether it has any hot spots. To find out, you will need to make a batch of cookie dough. Why not try this simple shortbread?

Put 100 g plain flour, 75 g butter and 25 g caster sugar into a food processor. Blitz until a dough is formed. Set the oven to 180°C/Gas mark 4. Cut the cookie dough into even-sized pieces and space out around two greased and lined baking trays. Bake for approximately 10 minutes. Carefully remove from the oven, remembering which tray was placed in which position in the oven. Note down any differences in colour between the cookies nearest the oven walls and those farthest from the walls. What do these results tell you about whether there are hot spots in your oven or not?

2   Why not produce a poster that explains cooking in a 'bain-marie' or 'water bath'.

VIDEO LINK

Watch the clip on how to make a really quick sponge cake in the microwave at www.brightredbooks.net/N5PCC

ONLINE TEST

How well have you learned this topic? Take the 'Chemistry of cooking' test at www.brightredbooks.net/N5PCC

THE BAKING PROCESS

When a mixture is baking, the heat travels through it, transforming it from a runny batter or dough into a baked product with a firm, dry outer crust and a softer centre. The soft centre consists of air cells supported by a structure that is made up of egg and gluten proteins embedded with starch and other particles.

1. FAT MELTS

One of the first things that happens when baked goods go into the oven is that solid fat melts. Most fats melt between 90°C and 130°C. As they melt, any trapped air and water escape from the fat. The water evaporates, creating steam. The steam then expands, pushing out the cell walls so that the baked goods start to rise. Butter has a low melting point and will provide a decent amount of air, especially if creamed well. However, some baking margarines might actually provide more air because they have higher melting points, meaning that the air escapes later, when there is more structure in place. Liquid oil contains no air or water so it definitely isn't a good choice of fat for a well risen sponge!

2. GASES FORM AND EXPAND

Three gases that are needed to help a baked product rise are air, steam and carbon dioxide. A cake or bread needs the heat from the oven to help the water present in the dough/mixture turn into steam. Heat also aids the **fermentation** of yeast, plus it activates the baking powder, which releases carbon dioxide. As the air bubbles get bigger and the gases expand, the cell walls are stretched.

3. SUGAR DISSOLVES

The heat of the oven means that sugar crystals dissolve into the batter or dough. As they dissolve, they can form sugar syrup and this can thin out the dough in the oven, causing it to spread. Be careful, therefore, not to add too much sugar. To prevent the cake mixture from collapsing, the structure needs to be properly in place.

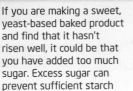

DON'T FORGET

If you are making a sweet, yeast-based baked product and find that it hasn't risen well, it could be that you have added too much sugar. Excess sugar can prevent sufficient starch gelatinisation.

4. COAGULATION AND GELATINISATION

The proteins in wheat (gluten) and egg (albumin) dry out and set when heat is applied. These proteins denature (strands of amino acids unravel) and then bond with one another, forming a structure that surrounds air cells. Starch present in the flour also has a part to play. The starch granules absorb water and begin to swell and burst at 170°C. **Gelatinisation** is usually complete at 200°C. The soft structure of the inside of a loaf of bread is mostly due to gelatinised starch. Very little starch gelatinisation occurs in cookie dough as there isn't enough water; hence a harder texture is achieved.

5. GASES EVAPORATE

As gases escape from baked goods, a dry hard crust forms on the surface due to the loss of moisture. Baked goods also lose weight as they lose moisture. Along with the gases comes the aroma that gives the baker the first indication that the baked product must soon be checked to see if it is ready.

When making bread, once the outer crust is formed, the bread can no longer expand. Some bakers add extra steam into the oven to help the surface of the bread to stay moist and thus the bread can continue to rise for a longer period of time, resulting in a less dense loaf of bread. You could do this at home by placing a baking tray with hot water in the bottom of the oven.

6. CARAMELISATION AND MAILLARD BROWNING OCCUR

The high baking temperature in the oven breaks down the molecules of sugar and protein on the surface of baked goods. This results in the formation of a brown colour and that lovely baked flavour that is missing when you microwave a cake. **Caramelisation** is the process of sugars breaking down. Maillard browning happens when sugars break down in the presence of protein.

7. COOLING

After you take your baked goods out of the oven, they continue to cook until they reach room temperature. This means you need to use your judgement to remove them from the oven just before they are baked to perfection.

DON'T FORGET

Most cookies are quite delicate when they are first taken out of the oven and therefore benefit from being left on the baking tray for a few minutes to firm up. Placing them onto a cooling rack to cool allows air to circulate around them, prevents moisture being trapped and therefore helps them to retain their crisp texture.

ONLINE TEST

How well have you learned this topic? Take the 'Baking process' test at www. brightredbooks.net/N5PCC

VIDEO LINK

Watch the spoof clip of the chemistry of baking a cake at www.brightredbooks. net/N5PCC. There are lots of YouTube clips of school science projects on the chemistry of cooking. Why not film your own version to show what chemical reactions take place when you prepare and bake a cake?

THINGS TO DO AND THINK ABOUT

Put together a flow chart that shows the chemical process that takes place when baking bread, cakes or cookies.

FUNCTION OF INGREDIENTS: FLOUR

ESSENTIAL INGREDIENTS

The quantities may differ, but the basic ingredients for baked goods are flour, fat, eggs and sugar.

FLOUR: AN OVERVIEW

There are many different types of flour available, but the flour most commonly used in cake making in the UK is wheat flour. Wheat is a cereal. It is milled to make flour.

When the grain is milled, the outer bran layer is removed. With white flour, more of the bran is removed than you will find in wholemeal flour. All flour contains between 70 and 80 per cent starch. By law, it must have iron, calcium and B vitamins added to replace those removed during the milling process.

The proteins found in wheat are called **gliadins** and **glutenins**. When water is added to flour these two proteins join together to make a stretchy, elastic substance known as **gluten**. Hard wheat produces strong flour, which has a high protein (gluten) content and is excellent for making bread. Soft wheat produces soft flour with less protein content. Flour should be sieved before use to remove any lumps, plus to add air.

MAIN TYPES OF FLOUR AND THEIR USES

There are many different types of flour. This table shows the main uses of the most important types of flour.

TYPE OF FLOUR	MAIN USES
Plain white flour	Contains approximately 10 per cent protein, with no added raising agent. Ideal for biscuits and pastries but can be used for cakes as long as raising agent is added.
Self-raising flour	Has a chemical raising agent added. Designed to be the correct amount for a light/medium sponge, but too much for rich mixtures with a lot of eggs/fat in them.
Wholemeal flour	Coarser in texture than white flour. It contains more bran and germ so is higher in insoluble fibre than white flour. It has a darker colour and a distinctly nutty flavour.
Granary flour	A mixture of white flour and rye flour with whole grains and malt extract added.
Strong white flour	Made from hard wheat, which has a high protein content providing lots of stretchy gluten which holds lots of air bubbles. Ideal for making bread and other products that contain yeast.
00 flour	Usually milled in Italy. This is a wheat flour that is generally is used to make pasta. Tends to be lower in protein/gluten than British white flour so will produce a finer texture in cakes.
Durum flour	Used to make pasta. It has a high protein content but isn't suitable to bake with as its gluten is tough and doesn't stretch.
Cornflour	Made from maize and is almost 100 per cent starch. It contains no gluten so is suitable for those suffering from coeliac disease.
Rice flour	Made from ground raw rice. It can be used to make cakes and biscuits but it is naturally gluten-free (check products for their gluten status as flours can become contaminated during milling).

Endosperm

Bran

Germ · A wheat kernel

The endosperm contains starch and proteins.
The germ is where a new plant will grow from.
The bran is the outside layer which covers the grain.

ONLINE

You can find out more about different types of flour via the BBC link at www.brightredbooks.net/N5PCC

VIDEO LINK

Check out the 'Grain Chain' link at www.brightredbooks.net/N5PCC for lots of different activities linked to finding out more about flour and grain, including how grain is made into flour.

DON'T FORGET

Flour is perishable. It must be kept in a cool, dry place. Sometimes flour kept past its use-by date can get infested by weevils - tiny beetles.

FUNCTIONAL PROPERTIES OF FLOUR

PROVIDING STRUCTURE

Gluten and starch are responsible for most of the structure-building ability of flour. When the dough is heated, the gluten is stretched by bubbles of gas produced by the raising agents. The gluten proteins **coagulate** – or set – producing a stable, risen product.

ABSORBING LIQUIDS

Starch in the flour absorbs moisture from the dough and **gelatinises**. This helps to produce moist baked products with a good texture.

FLAVOUR PROVIDER

Wheat flours have a relatively mild, slightly nutty flavour. Wholewheat flour provides the most flavour as it contains the germ and the bran.

COLOUR PROVIDER

Starch helps baked products to become brown. The breakdown of sugar and protein to provide the dark colour on crusts of baked products is called 'Maillard browning'. The greater the protein content, the greater the degree of browning.

ADDING NUTRITIONAL VALUE

Flour is a good source of energy and protein, and also of iron, calcium and B vitamins. These are added to fortify the flour after milling.

 ONLINE TEST

How well have you learned this topic? Take the 'Function of ingredients: flour' test at www.brightredbooks.net/N5PCC

 THINGS TO DO AND THINK ABOUT

1 By law, the government states wheat flour must be fortified with certain nutrients. The Food Standards Agency in Scotland recommends the mandatory **fortification** of wheat flour with folic acid. Undertake some research into this issue. Put together a presentation that highlights the pros and cons. What conclusions have you come to?

2 One of the best ways to find out more about the different types of flour is to experiment with making the same product, but using different types of flour. Why not use a basic sponge cake recipe (50 g margarine, 50 g caster sugar, 50 g flour and 1 egg). Make different batches using different types of flour. Once the cakes are made, evaluate your results.

Points of evaluation:
- Cut each cake in half. Measure the height to gauge how well it has risen.
- What does the texture look like? Are their lots of air bubbles visible?
- Rate the crust colour from light to dark.
- What is the flavour like?
- Finally, evaluate overall acceptability – which flour do you think has produced the best cake and which is the least acceptable?

3 1 in 100 people in the UK have coeliac disease, an autoimmune condition caused by intolerance to gluten. The only treatment for those with the condition is a strict gluten-free diet for life. Undertake some research into this condition. Once you understand more about it, develop a cake, biscuit or traybake that would be suitable for someone with coeliac disease.

Coeliac UK is the national charity for people with coeliac disease and dermatitis herpetiformis and provides expert advice and support for the 1 in 100 people with the condition.

FUNCTION OF INGREDIENTS: FAT AND EGGS

FAT: AN OVERVIEW

Butter and block margarine are the fats most commonly used for baking. White vegetable fat, lard and oil can also be used but low-fat spreads are not recommended as they break down when cooked at high temperatures.

Fats and oils are all classified as **lipids**. Fats are lipids that are solid at room temperature. Oils are lipids that are liquid at room temperature.

Butter is made from the cream from milk. The average block of butter is made up of 81 per cent fat, 16 per cent water, 2 per cent salt, 0.5 per cent protein and 0.5 per cent carbohydrate. Unsalted butter is the fat used most often when making rich fruit cakes. Unsalted butter provides a distinctive buttery flavour.

Margarine was invented in the 1860s by a French chemist as a cheap replacement for butter. Most margarines are made from soy bean oil but can be made from any vegetable fat. They are chemically hardened from a liquid oil via a process known as **hydrogenation**. This process is believed to convert the polyunsaturated fat into trans-fats which have a negative effect on cholesterol and are now thought to be linked to heart disease even more than saturated fat. By law, margarine must be fortified with vitamins A and D.

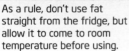

FUNCTIONAL PROPERTIES OF FAT

PROVIDING SHORTNESS

Fats and oils coat the structure builders in a cake (starch and protein), which prevents them from forming long strands. As the fat surrounds and coats the flour particles, it reduces the amount of water that can mix with the flour, so less gluten is produced. This gives baked goods that are high in fat a short, crumbly texture.

ADDING FLAVOUR

Butter in particular provides a distinct buttery flavour to baked goods.

FOAMING

When beaten or creamed, fat has the ability to trap air bubbles. This foam helps cakes to rise and have a light texture. Adding sugar into the fat when creaming allows lots of air to be trapped – a process known as **aeration**.

EXTENDING KEEPING QUALITIES

Fat helps baked products to retain their moisture so they don't dry out so quickly and will last longer.

NON-STICK

If the cooking container is greased with fat, this can help to prevent food from sticking to it.

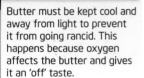

DON'T FORGET

As a rule, don't use fat straight from the fridge, but allow it to come to room temperature before using.

DON'T FORGET

Butter must be kept cool and away from light to prevent it from going rancid. This happens because oxygen affects the butter and gives it an 'off' taste.

ONLINE

Want to find out more about butter? Why not listen to the BBC radio programme discussing the decline and revival of butter-making at www.brightredbooks.net/N5PCC

ONLINE

Find out more about different types of fat via the BBC website. The link can be found at www.brightredbooks.net/N5PCC

VIDEO LINK

If you've never made butter before, why not give it a go? The 'Butter' link at www.brightredbooks.net/N5PCC will show you how! You could use the buttermilk to make scones or soda bread.

EGGS: AN OVERVIEW

When a recipe states one egg, this usually means a medium-sized egg. There are different types of egg sold, and what you use is a matter of personal preference. Caged eggs come from hens that have been kept in cages. Barn eggs are from hens that are free to roam within a barn. Free-range eggs are from hens that are allowed to roam free and eat a more natural diet.

Eggs should ideally be stored in a refrigerator with the round ends uppermost. They need to be allowed to come to room temperature before using.

Hens' eggs are made up of 10 per cent shell, 60 per cent white and 30 per cent yolk.

The shell is porous, which allows oxygen (but also bacteria) in. The air space is formed as the egg cools after the hen has laid it. The bigger the air space, the older the egg. This is why, when they are tested in water, older eggs float while fresher ones sink.

The **white** of an egg is predominantly made up of water and protein (albumin) and contains almost no fat. As the egg ages, the white gets thinner and it loses its ability to form a stable **foam** when whisked, so always aim to use eggs that are as fresh as possible when baking.

Egg yolk is made up of protein, fat and water, along with vitamins and minerals. It also contains lecithin, which is an **emulsifier** (allows oil and water to mix together). The colour of the egg yolk is related to the hen's diet, which will affect the taste of the egg. This does not, however, affect the nutritional value. As the egg gets older the yolk thins, making it more difficult to separate from the white.

FUNCTIONAL PROPERTIES OF EGGS

TRAPPING AIR

Both the egg white on its own and the whole egg can trap air due to the ability of the protein to stretch. One egg white can hold up to seven times its own volume in air. However, if beaten too much, the albumin will overstretch, release air and become liquid.

FOAMING

This allows eggs to lighten mixtures and produce a more open texture due to the addition of air. When whisking egg to form a foam, if it is left to stand, the foam will collapse and return to a liquid form. Fat reduces the volume of the foam, so there must be **no** egg yolk when whisking egg whites. Adding sugar increases the time it takes to produce the foam because it slows down the **denaturation** of the protein – hence the reason it's always best to whisk the egg white until it stands in peaks before adding any sugar.

ADDING STRUCTURE

When egg is heated, the protein sets (coagulates), giving structure to baked products.

ADDING NUTRITIONAL VALUE

Egg provides protein, vitamins and minerals (although the yolk does contain cholesterol).

CONTRIBUTING FLAVOUR

The rich flavour that eggs add to a product mostly comes from the yolk, which contains the fat.

PRODUCING A SHINY SURFACE

The protein in egg helps produce a glossy brown surface on the top of baked goods that are glazed with egg-wash.

DON'T FORGET

Eggs are best stored in a fridge, away from strong smelling foods. They should be removed from the fridge an hour or so before they are needed to be used, as cold eggs do not whisk well.

DON'T FORGET

When added to creamed mixtures, eggs must be at room temperature. If they are too cold, the mixture can curdle (meaning the fat will separate from the sugar and eggs when the eggs are added). Always crack them into a separate bowl before using to check they are OK, to prevent spoiling the cake mixture.

ONLINE

Want to find out more about eggs? Look at the links at www.brightredbooks.net/N5PCC

ONLINE TEST

How well have you learned this topic? Take the 'Function of ingredients: fat and eggs' test at www.brightredbooks.net/N5PCC

THINGS TO DO AND THINK ABOUT

A number of people suffer from an egg allergy. Children in particular are more likely to be allergic to eggs than adults. Your task is to produce a baked product that does not include egg. This might mean you using an egg substitute. For some ideas, check out http://www.egglesscooking.com/. There is a recipe for Eggless Fruit Cake on page 89 that you might want to try.

FUNCTION OF INGREDIENTS: SUGAR

Sugar cane

Sugar beet

VIDEO LINK

Watch the 'Jimmy's Food Factory' clip at www.brightredbooks.net/N5PCC to see how sugar is refined.

Honeycomb

SUGAR: AN OVERVIEW

There are a variety of different types of sugar that can be used in baking, and the key to successful baking is to have an understanding of each of them and what they can bring to your baked product. Strictly speaking, you should talk about using a sweetener in your product, not just sugar. Sweeteners refer to sugars, syrups and artificial sweeteners. Sugars are classified as simple carbohydrates, and are further broken down into **monosaccharides** (glucose and fructose), which are present in ripened fruits, and **disaccharides** (maltose, lactose, sucrose). When we think about sugar, we generally mean sucrose. Sucrose comes from sugar beet or sugar cane. White sugar and brown sugar have exactly the same sweetness levels – it's just the taste that can vary.

Sugar cane was first grown in the South Pacific thousands of years ago. Eighty per cent of sugar production comes from cane (in hot tropical climates) and 20 per cent from beet (in cooler climates). Freshly harvested sugar cane is first crushed to extract the juice. Water is evaporated off, leaving a thick golden syrup. The syrup is filtered and concentrated, resulting in the formation of sugar crystals. These crystals then produce a light brown crude raw sugar that is ready to be refined into white sugar. It goes through a lot of further processing before it reaches us as the sugar we use to bake with.

A syrup is a mixture of sugar dissolved in water. A simple syrup just involves heated sugar and water. Water is driven off and a syrup is formed. The ratio of sugar to water should not go above 2:1 or the sugar is likely to crystallise. (Adding a spot of lemon juice can help prevent this.)

Liquid syrups such as corn syrup, maple syrup and honey are sometimes called invert syrup. Invert syrup is sweeter than sugar and browns much faster, so when used in baked goods, the oven temperature needs to be turned down by a few degrees. Honey is sometimes called a natural invert syrup. It also browns easily and is very sweet, but it does keep baked items soft.

There are two types of artificial sweeteners: intense and bulk. Intense sweeteners – for example, saccharin, aspartame – are 300 and 2000 times sweeter respectively than sucrose. Bulk sweeteners – for example, sorbitol – are used in the same quantities as sugar.

MAIN TYPES OF SUGAR AND THEIR USES

There are many different types of sugar. This table shows the main uses of the most important types of sugar.

TYPE OF SUGAR	DESCRIPTION AND MAIN USES
Granulated sugar	Made from raw sugar extracted from cane/beet.
Caster sugar	Made the same way as granulated sugar but the process is modified so that it is milled so that much smaller crystals are obtained. Generally caster sugar is best for making sponge cakes.
Golden granulated/caster sugar	Goes through the same process, but not all the coloured impurities are removed in the refining process.
Soft brown sugar	Made by adding molasses back into refined white sugar. The darker the colour, the stronger the taste. It provides a cake with more moisture than white sugar.
Demerara sugar	Made from raw sugar treated with light-coloured molasses. The granules are larger than granulated sugar and pale brown in colour.
Muscovado sugar	Similar to Demerara sugar, but it contains more molasses and has a strong flavour. For rich fruit cakes, muscovado sugar gives a much richer, more treacly flavour.
Icing sugar	Obtained by crushing granulated sugar to a very fine powder in a special mill. An anti-caking agent is added to prevent the sugar going lumpy.
Preserving sugar	Granulated sugar that has pectin added to help the jam set.
Black treacle	Made from molasses. It is a thick, dark-coloured syrup with a strong distinctive flavour.
Molasses	A thick, dark, heavy syrup which is a by-product of sugar refining.
Golden syrup	An amber-coloured, thick sugar syrup made in the process of sugar making.

FUNCTIONAL PROPERTIES OF SUGAR

ADDING SWEETNESS

All sugars will add a sweet taste to baked goods, although not all to the same degree. Fructose is considered sweeter than sucrose, so watch out for this if you are using powdered fructose when baking. Powdered fructose is used in products such as nutrition bars, muffins and cookies.

IMPROVING SHELF LIFE

The ability of sugar to hold moisture also prolongs the shelf life of baked goods. Liquid sugars hold more moisture than other types of sugars, just as brown sugar will hold more moisture than granulated white sugar.

PROVIDING COLOUR AND FLAVOUR

When sugar is heated, it melts into a liquid and turns brown (called caramelisation). However, when making baked goods, Maillard browning also occurs due to the presence of protein in the cake mixture.

ADDING AIR

Sugar helps to make cakes rise. When creaming together fat and sugar, the sugar crystals cut into the fat, trapping air bubbles. Fine crystals in caster sugar give the best result, whereas icing sugar crystals are too fine to trap enough air.

IMPROVING TEXTURE

Because sugar is hygroscopic – that is, it attracts water molecules – it helps the texture of cakes or baked goods to feel nice and moist. It also helps them to remain that way as sugar takes up some of the water that would be absorbed by the protein, so gluten development is reduced.

INCREASED RISING

Sugar increases the coagulation temperature of the proteins in a cake mixture. This means that the gas cells in the mixture have more time to expand before setting, therefore giving a better rise to a cake.

THINGS TO DO AND THINK ABOUT

1   Think about making a cake or biscuits using honey as a substitute for sugar. For 50 g granulated sugar, use 50 g honey, but make sure you reduce the liquid content of the recipe by 10 g. Evaluate the product you make. How does it differ in taste/colour/texture to a similar product made using sugar?

2   Experiment with using different sweeteners to make a basic fairy cake or biscuit.

Record your results in a table:

Type of sugar	Crust colour	Sweetness	Flavour	Texture	Shape	Additional comments

3   Most people know that excess consumption of sugar is bad for you, but research has shown that eating a diet high in fructose could be even more harmful to health. Undertake some research into the pros and cons of fructose. Put a presentation together or produce a poster that explains what fructose is and why it could be so bad for your health.

ONLINE

Find out more about sugar via the BBC ingredients website. The link can be found at www.brightredbooks.net/N5PCC

DON'T FORGET

All sugars are hygroscopic – meaning that they attract and absorb water/moisture. This is great for keeping your cake moist. It is really important to store sugar in airtight containers to prevent them clumping together and becoming hard – a particular problem with soft brown sugar. If, on the other hand, you have covered a cake in sugarpaste, it's vital you do not seal it into an airtight box, but instead allow air to circulate around it as the icing will sweat, and any models you have already made and placed onto the cake will be in danger of getting spoiled.

DON'T FORGET

Once it has dissolved during the baking process, sugar causes cookie dough to spread. The sugar pulls water from the protein and starches present, turning the cookie dough into more of a sugar syrup. Sugar with a finer granule will dissolve sooner, so will spread more. Therefore, the more sugar you add to the cookie dough, the more the cookie spreads. **Do not** add extra sugar if you want your cookies to be successful!

ONLINE TEST

How well have you learned this topic? Take the 'Function of ingredients: sugar' test at www.brightredbooks.net/N5PCC

STORAGE AND PREPARATION OF ESSENTIAL INGREDIENTS

Effective baking actually begins long before a cake reaches the oven. Taking care of, and paying attention to, the preparation stages can make all the difference to the end result.

And remember – the final product is only as good as the component parts used to make it, so if you can, always try to buy good quality ingredients.

FLOUR

PREPARATION

Flour needs to be sieved before use. This will remove any lumps and add air.

STORAGE

To maximise the shelf life of your flour, place the bag of flour into a sturdy plastic bag. You can actually freeze for 48 hours which will kill off any weevils in the flour. Store in a sturdy plastic container with a tight fitting lid. Keep in a cool, dark place. By doing so, the flour should have a shelf life of around six months.

VIDEO LINK

Check out the clip at www.brightredbooks.net/N5PCC which shows how to store flour.

FAT

Fat adds moisture, flavour and keeping qualities to baked goods, but also add calories and can be bad for health. However, some baked goods just cannot be made without fat. Ideally, use unsalted butter in your recipes where possible.

PREPARATION

If the fat is to be used in a creamed mixture, take it out of the fridge and allow it to come to room temperature to soften first.

For rubbed-in mixtures, it's better to use the fat straight from the fridge and cut into small pieces with a knife to avoid handling with hot hands.

STORAGE

Fats and oils can develop 'off' (or rancid) flavours when exposed to heat, light and air – mostly from oxidation. To prevent oxidation/rancidity, keep out moisture and light by covering the fat tightly. Store butter in a fridge at 0–5°C. If wrapped in a plastic bag, butter can actually be stored in the freezer for six to nine months.

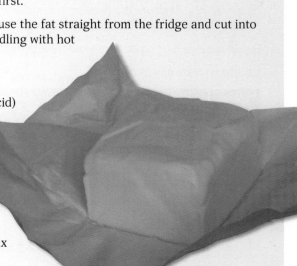

DON'T FORGET

Low-fat spreads contain a high water content and are generally not suitable for baking.

EGGS

PREPARATION

Recipes usually ask for eggs to be at room temperature before using. Cold eggs straight from the fridge do not whisk as well as eggs at room temperature, and therefore do not trap as much air. Eggs at room temperature also whisk up more quickly, as the protein in the whites is less elastic when cold.

You may find that a cold egg will not bind as well with other ingredients, so a batter can curdle, resulting in a flat cake.

Eggs tend to be easier to separate when cold, so use straight from the fridge if you plan to whisk egg white to make meringue. Remember, there must be **no** yolk in with the egg white, because the fat will inhibit the egg's ability to trap air.

Older egg white is thinner and will whip more easily to a greater volume than thicker, fresher white. However, once whipped, the foam from the older, thinner white is less stable, due to the liquid draining more easily from the bubbles. The rule of thumb is to use the freshest eggs possible for meringue.

STORAGE

Eggs should be kept at a constant temperature of below 20°C. Refrigerated, they will keep for approximately three to five weeks. Eggs can also be frozen, but **never** freeze whole eggs in their shells. Pierce the yolk and add a sprinkle of sugar (if it is to be used for sweet dishes) or salt (if it is to be used for savoury dishes).

SUGAR

PREPARATION

Sugar needs very little preparation before it is used in baked goods. You might need to sieve it to remove any lumps. It can be stirred into mixtures, creamed with fat to incorporate air, whisked with egg to trap air or melted and stirred into a mixture.

STORAGE

Sugar should ideally be stored in an airtight container. This not only helps to prevent the sugar picking up odours, but it also reduces the risk of the sugar absorbing moisture. This is particularly important with brown sugar, which tends to clump. To de-clump brown sugar, warm it gently in a microwave before passing it through a sieve.

Syrups with a high moisture content, such as maple syrup, should be stored in a fridge to prevent yeast and mould growth. It's best not to refrigerate other syrups as it can cause them to crystallise.

THINGS TO DO AND THINK ABOUT

1   To find out if your egg is fresh or stale, place the whole egg into a glass of water. If the egg is stale, it will float, and if it sinks, it is fresh. Use www.egginfo.co.uk to find out why this is the case.

2   Do some research into the proper procedures for handling and storing honey. Display your results in a poster.

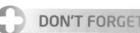

DON'T FORGET

Remove eggs from the fridge 30 minutes before using.

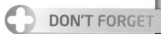

DON'T FORGET

If egg white needs to be warmed to reach room temperature, warm very gently over a hot water bath, stirring constantly. If overheated, the protein will coagulate and will not whip.

DON'T FORGET

All sugars are **hygroscopic** – that is, they pick up water from moist air, so they must be stored in a cool, dry place.

VIDEO LINK

Head to www. brightredbooks.net/N5PCC and watch the video clip on how to cream together butter and sugar.

ONLINE TEST

How well have you learned this topic? Take the 'Storage and preparation of essential ingredients' test at www. brightredbooks.net/N5PCC

STORAGE AND PREPARATION OF FRUIT AND CAKES

DON'T FORGET

Fresh fruit should be washed before use, but not washed before storage as water left on the fruit can encourage mould growth.

DON'T FORGET

Fruit was originally dried to preserve it. The most common dried fruit is raisins, which are dried grapes. Confused about the differences between currants, raisins and sultanas? Currants are dried, dark red seedless grapes. Raisins are dried white grapes. Sultanas are also dried white grapes, but from a seedless variety and tend to be sweeter and more golden in colour.

DON'T FORGET

Some fresh fruit such as apples begin to brown within minutes of being cut, due to exposure to oxygen – this is called **oxidisation**. Sprinkle with lemon juice to reduce this browning action.

DON'T FORGET

Before adding frozen fruit to a muffin or cake batter, coat the fruit with a light dusting of flour. This prevents the juice from the thawing fruit from mixing with the batter and discolouring it.

ONLINE

Head to www. brightredbooks.net/N5PCC and follow the 'Still Tasty' link to a website that tells you how long foods last and the best way to store them.

FRUIT

There is a huge range of fruit that can be incorporated into baked products. Fruit can be fresh, frozen, canned, dried and crystallised. Fruit adds flavour, colour and texture to baked goods. Before deciding what type of fruit is best to use, it is important that you consider your final product.

PREPARATION

Wash the fruit, peel if appropriate, dry and remove any stalks/cores. Slice or chop as required. Fruit must be dry to prevent it sticking. It's also a good idea to wash off any syrup coating, as this can cause fruit to sink in a cake. Some dried fruit might need to be soaked. Soaking stops the dried fruit pulling moisture from the mixture, preventing a dry cake.

STORAGE

Do not store fresh fruit in closed plastic bags. Fruits give off gas that causes them to ripen, so keeping fruit in a closed plastic bag prevents air from circulating and accelerates this process. Store ripe fruits at low temperatures so that they last longer. Avoid putting unripened fruits in a fridge as they won't ripen properly. Bananas suffer from chilling injury so mustn't be stored in the fridge.

Some fresh fruits give off ethylene gas and must be stored separately – for example – keep cherries away from peaches, and lemons away from apples. Dried fruits are best stored in a cool, dry place, in an airtight container.

STORING CAKES AND INGREDIENTS

Ingredients and baked products need to be stored correctly in appropriate packaging to extend shelf life, retain the quality and ensure they are safe to eat.

MARZIPAN AND FONDANT ICING

Unopened marzipan or fondant icing should be kept in cool, dry conditions away from sunlight. Once opened, they must be kept sealed to prevent them from drying out. Wrap tightly in several layers of cling film and store at room temperature.

Dr.Oetker

Marzipan
Ready to Roll

NO ADDED COLOUR

Perfect with Regal-Ice Icing

serving suggestion

contd

ROYAL ICING

You should cover royal icing with a damp cloth while you are working with it to prevent a crust forming. It should be stored in an airtight container. Place a layer of cling film onto the icing surface before putting on the lid to prevent any air getting to the icing. It can be placed in the fridge, but it doesn't have to be. It will need to be re-beaten to its original consistency every two days.

RICH FRUIT CAKE

You are best to store a rich fruit cake in the lining paper it was cooked in. The cake can be sprinkled with some alcohol before being wrapped in a few layers of greaseproof paper. This type of rich cake must not be stored in an airtight plastic container as it can sweat and encourage mould growth. It can be placed in a cardboard box or wrapped in foil – but it is important that the aluminium foil is **not** placed directly onto the cake as it can react with the fruit acids and can disintegrate. This type of cake matures with keeping, but is probably best eaten within three months.

UNDECORATED CAKES

Undecorated cakes are best stored in an airtight container. The keeping quality of cakes depends upon the individual mixture. Fatless sponge cakes such as Swiss roll quickly become dry, so should be eaten within one to two days. A Victoria Sandwich cake will keep in an airtight container for approximately one week.

DECORATED CAKES

Once a cake has been marzipaned and iced it must be stored in a cardboard box. Avoid damp and cold conditions as this can cause the icing to stain and colourings to run. **Do not** store in an airtight box as the decoration can sweat.

> **DON'T FORGET**
>
> Most cakes that are not decorated freeze well. They are best frozen undecorated, sealed in an airtight plastic bag or wrapped in cling film.

THINGS TO DO AND THINK ABOUT

1 Make a basic muffin batter. Try adapting the recipe by adding the same variety of fruit, but change it to include fresh, dried, and frozen versions. Evaluate your results. Which do you prefer and why?

2 Produce a poster that gives 'Dos and Don'ts' when storing different cakes. Include a timescale for how long each cake can be expected to last if stored appropriately.

> **ONLINE TEST**
>
> How well have you learned this topic? Take the 'Storage and preparation of fruit and cakes' test at www. brightredbooks.net/N5PCC

PREPARATION OF EQUIPMENT

CHOOSING YOUR CAKE TIN

Choosing and preparing your cake tin well can make all the difference between a successful, perfectly shaped cake and a misshapen disappointment.

Cake tins come in many different shapes and sizes. It is worth investing in good quality cake tins, which will last for years if looked after properly. The size given in the recipe is for the measurement across the base of the tin. If you want to use a different cake tin to the one stated in the recipe, then make sure that it has the same capacity. You can use water to check this. So, for example, if the recipe asks you to use a 16 cm round cake tin, fill it up with water and then pour the water into the tin you want to use instead, until it is full. That will allow you to gauge how much quantity your new tin will take and will let you know if you need to adapt your recipe quantities in any way.

A good rule to use is: the larger the tin, the thinner the cake will be and the less cooking time it will require. And if you would rather use a square tin instead of a round tin, go down a size – for example, if the recipe states 20 cm round, then the mixture should fit well into an 18 cm square tin.

SUCCESSFUL LINING

Medium-sized cakes or light fruit cakes that do not require many hours in the oven will cope with a single layer of greaseproof paper lining. However, larger cakes and most rich fruit cakes that are in the oven for a number of hours will need extra protection. You could consider buying pre-shaped greaseproof paper liners that come in different shapes and sizes. These save time and effort, but can be more expensive to buy.

The following equipment is required for successful lining:

- greaseproof paper
- pencil
- scissors
- pastry brush
- string
- brown paper/newspaper
- fat or oil.

FAT FOR GREASING

The most convenient fat to use for greasing is **oil**. Placing oil into an atomiser is a great way of spraying on a small amount of oil exactly where you need it.

Lard or white fat is suitable for greasing, but try to avoid butter and margarine due to possible salt content and higher water content. Butter also burns at a lower temperature.

contd

THREE MAIN WAYS TO PREPARE TINS

1   If you are using a baking tray to cook biscuits, or a patty tin for pastry cases, lightly grease the tray with oil. Some recipes ask you to dust the tray lightly with flour after greasing. This provides an extra bit of insurance. Depending upon your recipe, the flour can help keep the caramelised sugar from sticking to the pan. Flour also creates a barrier between the oil and the mixture to prevent the oil seeping into the mixture.

2   For whisked sponges, such as Swiss roll, the tin should be greased lightly and lined with paper. It's important not to add too much oil as the fat can affect the foam's ability to rise and it can end up stuck to the paper. Lightly grease and flour the inside of the tin to prevent the mixture sticking. Place the tin on top of a piece of greaseproof paper that is 2.5 cm larger than the tin to be lined. Cut diagonally from the corner of the paper to the corner of the tin. This allows the corners to overlap and fit the tin neatly.

3   For rubbed-in and creamed mixtures, grease the tin with oil before lining the tin on the base. Be sure to lightly grease the paper before adding the mixture. Depending upon the cake, it might need the sides of the tin to be greased and lined. For cakes that require longer cooking, such as rich fruit cake, tins are best lined with double thickness. You should also line tins around the outside to prevent the outside crust from getting overcooked/dry.

TIN LINING

Draw round the base of the tin. Cut out the circle of greaseproof paper. Grease the base of the tin. Line with the circle of paper. Grease on top.

To line both the base and the sides with double thickness paper draw around the base of the tin. This time cut out two pieces. Grease the base and sides before adding the first square of greaseproof onto the base. Grease on top of the paper.

Use a piece of string to measure a length of greaseproof that will wrap around the whole tin. Make sure the strip is doubled over. The paper should stand approximately 2–3 cm above the top of the tin. Snip along the bottom edge of the paper. Insert this into the tin. Grease before adding the second square on the base.

  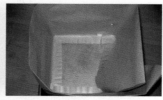

VIDEO LINK

Head to www. brightredbooks.net/N5PCC and check out the clip that will show you how to prepare the tin for your Christmas cake.

DON'T FORGET

If you are a beginner baker, think about starting off with a round Christmas cake. It's much easier to line a round cake tin than it is a square tin. It takes a bit more practice to get the paper into the corners to give you a sharp edge when a square cake is baked.

DON'T FORGET

As well as preparing your tin before baking, remember to think about whether you need to adjust the oven shelves for the cake you are making. For example, a Madeira cake needs to be placed on a shelf one third from the bottom of the oven.

ONLINE TEST

How well have you learned this topic? Take the 'Preparation of equipment' test at www.brightredbooks. net/N5PCC

TOP TIP

Tying brown paper around the outside of the tin, and securing with string, helps to protect the cake during a long, slow cooking process.

THINGS TO DO AND THINK ABOUT

Practice preparing both a round and a square cake tin for a rich fruit cake. Work with a partner and take a series of photos to use for a poster/leaflet. Or film the process.

PROCESSING TECHNIQUES: MAKING BAKED PRODUCTS 1

Outcome 2 of the Cake Baking Unit requires you to bake a range of cakes and other items by following recipe methods to achieve the **correct consistency** when incorporating the ingredients, **depositing** the mixture appropriately, **controlling the oven temperature**, **baking correctly** and carrying out **readiness tests**.

If you follow the instructions carefully, measure ingredients properly and use the correct method of mixing ingredients, you should achieve high quality baked products. Each step in the recipe is designed to encourage the combined action of the gluten (protein in flour) and the gases (carbon dioxide, air and steam) in the dough or batter, which help the cake to rise. Although the ingredients are very similar, the proportion of each and the way they are combined are different. These two factors result in baked products that vary in appearance, texture and flavour.

DON'T FORGET

The muffin/melted method relates to making American muffins. English muffins are made using yeast and are cooked on a griddle. American muffins need to be cooked in a deeper muffin tin to allow the mixture to rise. A cake patty tin isn't deep enough for a muffin mixture.

VIDEO LINK

Head to www.brightredbooks.net/N5PCC and watch the video clip showing muffins being made.

DON'T FORGET

A **batter** is a mixture of flour and liquid, usually combined with other ingredients. The mixture can be stirred with a spoon and is thin enough to pour or drop from a spoon. **Dough** on the other hand is a mixture of flour and liquid, usually with other ingredients added. A dough is thick enough to knead or roll and is too stiff to stir or pour.

INCORPORATING INGREDIENTS

Here are two of the main methods of incorporating ingredients:

- muffin/melted method
- rubbed-in/biscuit method.

MUFFIN/MELTED METHOD

Sieve the dry ingredients together in a large bowl. Mix (or melt) the liquid ingredients together in a separate bowl. Make a well (a hole) in the dry ingredients and pour in the liquid (or melted) ingredients. Stir only until the dry ingredients are moistened. The mixture should look like a slightly runny batter, and could have lumps if fruit is being used. **Do not overmix!** Gently fold in fruit or other ingredients.

Caution: Overmixing results in the muffins having a flat top, low volume, being tough and unevenly browned. Your muffins should have an even grain and a bumpy top.

To make it easier to deposit the batter into the prepared tin, consider pouring it first into a measuring jug so you can easily control how much mixture gets added to each space/paper case. Alternatively, an ice cream scoop will allow you to scoop an even amount of mixture into every case.

contd

RUBBED IN/BISCUIT METHOD

Sieve the dry ingredients together in a large bowl. Cut the fat into the dry ingredients. Rub in until the mixture resembles fine breadcrumbs. Add the liquid in small amounts at a time and gently press against the side of the bowl with a round bladed knife. When the dough forms a soft ball, knead gently for about 20 seconds to blend all the ingredients.

Caution: Adding the liquid too quickly will result in your mixture being dry. Consequently, you will have to add extra liquid, which will affect the quality of your final product.

Biscuits should be deposited onto a prepared baking tray in even-sized pieces. Try to handle the dough as little as possible to avoid a tough end result. They should be given enough space to allow them to spread/rise.

There are lots of different types of biscuits/cookies and each varies in terms of how it is prepared/deposited prior to baking.

TYPE OF BISCUIT/COOKIE	METHOD OF DEPOSITING MIXTURE
Drop cookie – for example, chocolate chip cookies	Made from a soft dough that is dropped from spoonfuls onto the baking tray.
Rolled cookie – for example, almond cookies	Made from a soft dough that generally gets rolled and cut before being placed onto the baking tray.
Piped cookie – for example, Viennese whirls	Pipe straight onto the tray. The mixture needs to be a soft enough consistency to pipe, but firm enough to keep its shape during baking.
Moulded cookie – for example, shortbread petticoat tails	Press into a greased mould, turn out and chill before placing onto baking tray. The dough needs to be soft – not dry or sticky.
Bar cookie – for example, brownie	Bar cookies are a cross between a cake and a cookie. A brownie mixture will be a slightly runny batter and needs to be poured into a prepared rectangular tin. Other bar cookies involve a soft dough being spread into the pan, and could consist of several layers.

VIDEO LINK

Ever tried using a cookie press? Watch the video at www.brightredbooks.net/N5PCC to see how simple it can be. Not got a cookie press? Don't worry – you can make similar shapes by using a piping bag – there's another clip showing you how in the Digital Zone.

ONLINE TEST

How well have you learned this topic? Take the 'Processing techniques: making baked products 1' test at www.brightredbooks.net/N5PCC

THINGS TO DO AND THINK ABOUT

Experiment with making your own batch of pressed or piped cookies. Why not try different flavours such as vanilla, chocolate, coffee, lemon or mixed spice? Be creative with your decoration – either before or after baking. For example, you could use chocolate chips, nuts, cherries, chopped fudge or chocolate drops. Evaluate your results. Which cookie looks and tastes best? Why is this the case?

PROCESSING TECHNIQUES: MAKING BAKED PRODUCTS 2

DON'T FORGET

Be very gentle when depositing a whisked fatless sponge mixture out of the bowl into the prepared tin as rough handling of the mixture will result in loss of air. Move the tray about gently to get the mixture into the corners – do not spread it in!

DON'T FORGET

Once rich fruit cake has been deposited into the tin, it needs to be 'dipped' on the surface to help the cake achieve a flat top.

VIDEO LINK

Watch a rich fruit cake being prepared at www. brightredbooks.net/N5PCC.

INCORPORATING INGREDIENTS CONTINUED

The creamed-cake method is the third main method of incorporating ingredients.

CREAMED-CAKE METHOD

Sieve the dry ingredients (except sugar) together in a bowl. Cream the softened fat with a wooden spoon or with an electric mixer. Add the sugar and continue creaming until the mixture is light and fluffy. (This change in colour shows that air has been successfully incorporated.) Add the eggs with a little of the flour and continue beating. Gently fold in the remaining dry ingredients. Flavourings, nuts and fruit can be folded in at end. The mixture should have a 'dropping' consistency – that is, it falls off the wooden spoon back into the bowl. Your cake should have a fine, even grain and a smooth top.

When spooning sponge mixture from the bowl into the prepared patty tin, it's a good idea to use your pinkie finger to scoop the mixture off the metal spoon; this avoids sticky mixture getting all over your hands!

A spatula or bowl scraper can be used to get every last bit of mixture out of the bowl. The mixture in the tin can be levelled off using the spatula or a metal spoon.

TECHNIQUES

- **Beat:** to make a mixture smooth either by using a brisk over and over motion with a wooden spoon or a wire balloon whisk, or by using a rotary motion with an electric mixer.

- **Blend:** to combine two or more ingredients until they are soft and smooth.

- **Cream:** to soften a fat with a spoon or mixer, either before or while mixing it with another food – usually sugar. When creaming fat and sugar, the sugar grains are cut into the fat with the purpose of trapping air.

- **Fold:** to blend delicate ingredients gently by using two motions – one to cut vertically through the mixture (usually with a rubber spatula), and the other to turn the mixture over onto itself by sliding the rubber spatula across the bottom of the mixing bowl, bringing it up the side and folding over on the top (usually a figure of eight cutting action). You can also fold using a metal spoon or a balloon whisk.

VIDEO LINK

Watch the creaming technique at www. brightredbooks.net/N5PCC

VIDEO LINK

See the folding technique for yourself at www. brightredbooks.net/N5PCC

contd

- **Incorporate:** to mix in any new ingredient so that it is evenly distributed throughout the mixture.
- **Knead:** to work a dough with your hands using a pressing motion followed by a folding motion.
- **Mix:** to combine ingredients in any way that causes a distribution.
- **Rub in:** to distribute small pieces of solid fat evenly through dry ingredients, usually using the fingertips to rub the mixture together. Again, used to trap air.
- **Stir:** to mix ingredients with a circular motion to blend them or make a uniform consistency.
- **Whip:** to beat rapidly to incorporate air and increase volume of the mixture. Eggs and cream are the foods most often whipped.

COOKING TEMPERATURES

Baking times vary with different recipes – even for the same product. It's important that you get to know your oven, and you might even want to use an oven thermometer to check if it needs adjusting. Always allow time to pre-heat the oven – it takes approximately 10 minutes to reach 180°C. Remember that you might need to make an adjustment for a fan oven. Cakes are usually best cooked in the centre of the oven, unless the recipe dictates otherwise. It's important not to overload the oven as this can lower the temperature and affect the end results.

TESTS FOR READINESS

The first thing to do is to make sure you follow the timing given in the recipe. Always take a note of the time when the product goes into the oven.

The appearance of a cake will vary according to its type – for example, you would expect a sponge cake to look well risen but this wouldn't be the case with a rich fruit cake.

PRODUCT	TEST FOR READINESS
Cookies/ biscuits	Remove from the oven as soon as the edges are golden, but the middle is a little pale. This will give a slightly chewy centre. For a crispy cookie, wait until the whole cookie is very lightly browned. Even if you think the cookie is too pale, check the bottom to make sure it is lightly browned. If so, it's ready.
Sponge cake	The mixture should have risen to the top of the tin and it should have almost doubled in volume. It should be evenly light golden-brown in colour. The cake should have shrunk away from the sides of the tin slightly and should bounce back if pressed lightly on top.
Fruit cake	Fruit cake should feel firm to touch and be well-browned in colour. A clean skewer should be inserted into the centre of the cake. Leave for a few seconds before removing. The cake is ready if there is no wet, sticky mixture clinging to the skewer. If the mixture is wet, but the top of the cake is brown, protect it from burning when the cake goes back into the oven by covering the top of the cake with greaseproof paper or foil.

THINGS TO DO AND THINK ABOUT

1 Class Challenge – set a timed challenge where students are all asked to prepare the same size and shape of cake tin. Points are given for speed and accuracy. The overall winner has the best prepared tin in the shortest time.

2 Select a suitable recipe to make a 15 cm cake that can be served for afternoon tea. Maximum flavour should come from the cake itself, not ingredients added to decorate it.

ONLINE

Check out the link about rubbing in at www.brightredbooks.net/N5PCC

ONLINE

Learn more about kneading by following the link at www.brightredbooks.net/N5PCC

ONLINE

See how to whip cream correctly by following the link at www.brightredbooks.net/N5PCC

DON'T FORGET

Imagine you had to bake at high altitude. The atmospheric pressure is lower, which makes liquid boil faster and causes greater evaporation, so you'd have to add more liquid to your mixture. You'd also have to increase your oven temperature the higher up you went!

DON'T FORGET

The richer the mixture, the cooler the oven.

VIDEO LINK

Watch Mary Berry demonstrating how to test a cake for readiness at www.brightredbooks.net/N5PCC

ONLINE TEST

How well have you learned this topic? Take the 'Processing techniques: making baked products 2' test at www.brightredbooks.net/N5PCC

BAKING TRENDS

VIDEO LINK

The Great British Bake Off, series 4, episode 9: French week saw the remaining contestants tackling canapés. Follow the link at www.brightredbooks.net/N5PCC to view the episode.

VIDEO LINK

The 'Doughnuts' video clip at www.brightredbooks.net/N5PCC shows how to make a basic doughnut.

VIDEO LINK

The clip at www.brightredbooks.net/N5PCC shows you how to make a basic biscuit. Think about how you could adapt the basic recipe to make your own modern flavour combination. Carry out some peer assessment of your finished biscuit.

ONLINE

Find out more about a gluten-free diet from the article at www.brightredbooks.net/N5PCC

VIDEO LINK

The clips at www.brightredbooks.net/N5PCC show how to assemble a checkerboard cake and how easy it can be to make marshmallow.

DON'T FORGET

Gelatine is used as a setting agent. It comes from **collagen** from animal by-products, so is not suitable for vegans.

BRIEF HISTORY OF BAKING

1900s	Girls were taught cookery in schools and Colleges of Domestic Science.
1920s	Women encouraged to take up home baking as a source of extra income.
1930s	Banana cake first appeared in recipe books as an ideal way to avoid food waste.
1940s	Rationing meant that Dripping Cake was a popular option.
1950s	Sugar was rationed until 1953 so golden syrup, treacle and condensed milk were used to satisfy a sweet tooth.
1980s	In an age of convenience, traybakes were a simple way of producing a cake in a hurry.
1990s	Cupcake wedding cakes first appeared.
2000s	Luxury cupcakes became the 'must have' cake.
2014	More people than ever are baking.

WHAT'S NEXT?

Cupcakes are still popular, but whoopee pies and macaroons have definitely had their day. So what's the next big thing to hit the bakery market? The following are possible contenders:

MINI PORTION SIZES – CANAPÉS

Canapés are small, decorative finger foods, usually eaten in one bite. Although they are traditionally savoury, there is a growing trend for bite-sized sweet canapés, because they appeal to health-conscious consumers.

DOUGHNUTS

This fried dough confectionary was traditionally served in a ring shape, but the round ball shape allows bakers to be creative and fill it with a range of new flavour combinations – not just jam or apple any more. New filling ideas include salted caramel, chilli mango, apricot cardamom and lemon meringue pie.

SWEET AND SAVOURY FLAVOUR COMBINATIONS IN CAKES AND BISCUITS

There is a growing market for bolder, gutsier flavours in cakes, cookies and biscuits. Some more unusual combinations include: vanilla, pecan and crushed crisps cookies; apricot and sage cookies; honey and harissa cake; chilli, ginger and lime biscuits and butterscotch toffee crunch cake.

GROWING DEMAND FOR GLUTEN-FREE PRODUCTS

It looks like it's not just those suffering from coeliac disease (gluten intolerance) that are buying gluten-free baked goods, but many consumers consider gluten-free goods to be healthier. This might not actually be the case, but the fact they think they are eating something that's better for them means more cakes and biscuits made from alternative grains are being produced than ever before.

PEEK-A-BOO CAKES

Peek-a-boo cakes are all about the surprises waiting inside when the cake is cut. Outside they look like any other cake that is covered in sugarpaste and decorated, but hidden inside could be a coloured checkerboard of sponge, bright red hearts or a carrot-shaped cake carved into plain sponge.

 contd

MARSHMALLOWS

Marshmallows are a sticky, soft, melt-in-the-mouth confection that can incorporate a huge range of colours and flavours to suit all tastes.

ZEBRA CAKE

Zebra cake is just the updated version of the marbled cake. To achieve the stripes successfully, you need to ensure that the different coloured cake mixtures are the same consistency. Work quickly as you pour them in layers into the prepared cake tin. It's an ideal cake to experiment with different colours and flavours.

ICED ECLAIRS

Once you've mastered choux pastry, the sky's the limit in terms of what you can do to jazz up the basic éclair. Experiment with coloured fondant or glace icing. Add some plunged flowers. Once you've cracked your technique, get experimenting with the cream filling, by adding hazelnut or almond extract, coffee or cocoa, lemon or lime.

RETRO CAKES

Classic no-bake traybakes are making a comeback. Nanaimo bars originate from Western Canada and are made up of a crunchy, coconut base, topped with a vanilla custard layer and finally topped with plain dark chocolate. Rocky Road makes use of marshmallows – another top baking trend ingredient.

CAKETAILS (COCKTAIL-INFUSED CAKES)

Although originally developed for cocktail parties, these highly flavoured creations can be made using mocktail mixtures. Alcohol-free mocktail mixtures can be used to flavour the sponge mixture, or added to the frosting for additional flavour. Try mojito, strawberry daiquiri or perhaps cherry cola flavour. An ideal cake to experiment with flavour and colour combinations!

OMBRE COLOUR

Finally, let's look at **Ombre Colour**. 'Ombre' means colour that's graduated from light to dark. It can have a stunning effect – and it's a currently trending in the fashion world with dip-dye hair and ombre dresses, skirts and tops. The effect can be fairly easily achieved in cakes – just take care when mixing in the food colouring!

VIDEO LINK

Head to www.brightredbooks.net/N5PCC and watch the clip which shows you how to deposit the batter into the prepared tin to make a Zebra Cake.

VIDEO LINK

Not sure how to make successful choux pastry? Watch the clip at www.brightredbooks.net/N5PCC

DON'T FORGET

To be successful at making choux pastry, you must make sure the water is boiling and that the flour is tipped into the pan all at the same time. You'll know you've got it right if the ball of paste comes away from the sides of the pan.

DON'T FORGET

Chocolate should be melted very carefully – watch the clip to see how it's done safely at www.brightredbooks.net/N5PCC

ONLINE TEST

How well have you learned this topic? Take the 'Baking trends' test at www.brightredbooks.net/N5PCC

THINGS TO DO AND THINK ABOUT

If you don't have time to make doughnuts from fresh, why not think about how you could decorate a basic ring doughnut to bring it right up to date with current trends?

Undertake some research to find gluten-free cake recipes. Select a suitable recipe for mini fairy cakes. Make, bake and evaluate your gluten-free cakes.

Try the amazing Snowflake Marshmallow recipe at www.brightredbooks.net/N5PCC to make some fabulous festive edible gifts.

EVALUATING BAKED ITEMS

EVALUATING: AN OVERVIEW

Outcome 2 in the Cake Baking unit asks you to evaluate the baked items you have made. This means that you will have to appraise or judge what's good about your product and what improvements you would make to it. Most importantly, you must state **why** you have come to these conclusions. You will be required to provide at least one evaluative statement for each of a range of aspects relating to the baked item, including:

- its appearance
- its texture
- its taste.

When you evaluate baked products, you will need to use the following senses: sight, touch, smell and taste.

You will also need to be aware of the standard quality characteristics of the product you have made, so that you have something to evaluate it against. The following table gives some basic quality criteria for some common baked goods.

BAKED PRODUCT	APPEARANCE	TEXTURE	FLAVOUR
Muffin	Rough pebbled surface, golden brown, slightly rounded top	Fairly large gas holes, evenly distributed	Basic plain muffin can be slightly bland
Victoria sponge cake	Golden brown, rounded top	Moist, light but not crumbly, small, even-sized air cells	Delicate, sweet flavour. Perhaps slight taste of egg or butter
Fatless sponge	Thin, golden brown crust	Light, well-aerated, melt-in-the-mouth	Not eggy
Biscuits	Uniform shape and colour	May be soft or crisp or chewy depending upon recipe	Will depend upon recipe used
Fruit cake	Slightly rounded top, good colour, slight gloss	Moist but not wet	Fruity, caramel-type flavour with hint of spice

APPEARANCE

This refers to the size, shape, colour and condition of the outside surface as well as the interior colour of the baked product. What should it look like? Compare this to what your final product does look like.

Some shape sensory terms that you could use include: round, oval, symmetrical, bulges, round on top, peaked, lopsided, well-shaped, level top, irregular, thin, sunken.

Some colour sensory terms that you could use include: browned, creamy colour, yellowish, grey, streaky, golden brown, burnt, spotty, black, lacking colour, mottled.

TEXTURE

This refers to the product structure. The size of the gas holes, thickness of cell walls and crumb texture. Consider how the food feels when it is in your mouth.

Some texture sensory terms that you could use include: crunchy, smooth, creamy, tough, tender, crumbly, soggy, crispy, soft, hard, moist, lumpy, fine, elastic, velvety, flaky, dry, springy, compact, heavy, light, rubbery, slimy, chewy.

TASTE

This refers to the aroma of the product as well as the flavour.

Some flavour sensory terms that you could use include: mild, strong, spicy, delicate, sweet, salty, sour, bitter, nut-like, unpleasant, flat, pleasant, characteristic of an ingredient or spice such as chocolate or cinnamon, eggy, yeasty, bland, burnt, buttery, fruity.

The following is an example of some points you could include in an evaluation.

EVALUATION

GOOD POINTS	PHOTOGRAPH OF MY BAKED ITEM	IMPROVEMENTS
Appearance My cake was a nice golden brown colour, as I made sure I checked the baking time and took it out of the oven before it got too brown. **Texture** My cake had quite a close texture as can be seen from the lack of big air bubbles which means I should perhaps have taken more time to cream the mixture. **Flavour** My cake tasted really quite fruity due to the addition of the cherries.		• I don't like the big cherries on the top of the cake, so next time I will mix them through the cake mix and not just place on top. • It doesn't look as if I have enough cherries as you can only see a few pieces on the base of the cake, so I should perhaps have added more. • The cherries have sunk to the bottom as I forgot to coat them in flour. I'll need to remember to do this next time.

Some points to consider when you are doing your product evaluations:

- Are you happy with the ingredients you chose? What might you change next time?
- Did you get the weighing/measuring/proportion of ingredients correct?
- How was the consistency of your cake mixture?
- Do you think you chose the correct size of tin in relation to the quantity of mixture and your chosen design?
- Is the surface of your cake level? Should you have made a well/dip prior to cooking?
- What do you think about your overall design?
- Is the colour of the product what you expected? Did you cook it for long enough or too long?
- Did you choose the correct tin to cook your baked product in? Would another shape have looked better?

THINGS TO DO AND THINK ABOUT

Take time to do some research into what the main quality characteristics are for the categories of cakes that you will have to make as part of your course. Draw up your own chart so that you can use it when you come to evaluating your own baked products.

 DON'T FORGET

A good way to make sure you have given an evaluative comment, and not just a statement, is to think about including a **Fact**, an **Opinion** and a **Consequence** – for example, I don't think that the cake's appearance is as good as I'd hoped (**O**) as I forgot to coat the cherries in flour (**F**) so they sank to the bottom (**C**).

 VIDEO LINK

Watch the clip on how to go about evaluating a baked product at www.brightredbooks.net/N5PCC

 ONLINE TEST

How well have you learned this topic? Take the 'Evaluating baked items' test at www.brightredbooks.net/N5PCC

FAULT FINDING

Even though you might have followed your recipe to the letter, sometimes things go wrong in cake-making. Don't worry! Look at the suggestions below to find out where you might have gone wrong, work out the particular issue that has affected your cake and try making it again, taking account of the possible solution.

CAKE HAS SUNK

- Perhaps you opened the oven door a few times during cooking, especially in the initial stages before the cake structure had time to set.

- Did you take the cake out of the oven before it was tested for readiness and perhaps wasn't fully cooked?

- Are you sure you included all of the ingredients or did you forget one?

- Did you use too much baking powder? Too much will mean the cake will rise too quickly and then sink.

- The fat and sugar might have been beaten for too long – was the fat too soft and almost runny when you started creaming?

- If the cake had too much liquid or too little flour it could have caused it to sink.

- Did you add too much sugar by mistake? Too much sugar can cause the gluten to collapse.

DON'T FORGET

Baking Powder is a raising agent. It is made from an alkali – bicarbonate of soda – and an acid – cream of tartar – plus a filler like cornflour or rice flour, which absorbs moisture. The powder is activated when liquid is added, producing carbon dioxide gas that causes the mixture to expand. For this reason, it is important to get your cake mixture into the oven quickly once the 'wet' ingredients have been added to the 'dry' ingredients.

CAKE HASN'T RISEN

- The oven temperature could have been too low or perhaps it was turned off accidentally.

- Perhaps you used insufficient raising agent.

- Perhaps plain flour was used instead of self-raising.

- Were you making a whisked sponge and the air was knocked out when folding in the flour?

- Did you spend enough time creaming the fat and sugar to trap air?

CAKE IS CRACKED ON TOP

- The oven was probably too hot.

- Did you remember to adjust the oven temperature to take account of the fan-assistance?

- The cake might have been baked on too high an oven shelf.

- Perhaps you didn't cream the fat and sugar enough.

- If the tin was too small for the amount of mixture, it could cause the cake to crack on top as it rises.

FRUIT IN THE CAKE HAS SUNK TO THE BOTTOM

- There could have been too much liquid in the cake, making it too wet to support the fruit.
- If cherries are left coated in syrup, they will sink. Did you remember to wash them and coat them in some flour?
- Your oven might have been too cool, so your cake might have cooked too slowly.

CAKE IS TOO DRY

- There is a good chance you didn't have enough liquid in your sponge mixture.
- Was the cake overcooked? Baking for too long will definitely dry it out.
- A dry texture could mean far too much raising agent was used.

CAKE HAS A SUGARY CRUST

- Fat and sugar may not have been creamed together for long enough.
- There is a good chance you used too much sugar in the mixture.
- It might be that the sugar used wasn't fine enough – for example, did you use granulated when the recipe said caster?

CAKE HAS A HEAVY TEXTURE

- There is a good chance that the mixture contained too much liquid. Remember, this might be because you used large eggs, not necessarily that you didn't measure the liquid correctly.
- You might have used too little raising agent.
- Did the mixture curdle when you were mixing it? If you added egg that was very cold, it could have cooled the fat down. The fat then gets surrounded by water which makes it difficult for the egg yolk to emulsify – basically meaning the mixture will hold less air.
- Did you check the oven temperature? It could have been too cool.
- Overbeating the mixture can cause a heavy texture in a sponge.

VIDEO LINK

Find out about early raising agents by watching the clip from The Great British Bake Off at www.brightredbooks.net/N5PCC

ONLINE

For some additional advice on what might have gone wrong with your cake, check out the link at www.brightredbooks.net/N5PCC

ONLINE TEST

How well have you learned this topic? Take the 'Fault finding' test at www.brightredbooks.net/N5PCC

THINGS TO DO AND THINK ABOUT

Develop a series of posters that highlight some of the main faults that can happen with cakes, and what to do to prevent these faults from happening.

FILLINGS AND COATINGS 1

The Cake Finishing unit requires you to prepare for finishing cakes and other baked items by selecting suitable fillings and coatings. You will have to use the fillings and coatings listed below:

- Buttercream/frosting
- Cream
- Chocolate/ganache
- Jams/curds
- Marzipan/almond paste
- Royal icing
- Sugarpaste

Adding a filling and a coating to a cake can make it more attractive and, of course, adds to the taste. It is, however, important to remember that if the cake has many layers plus an outer coating, this can make it very sweet.

DON'T FORGET

Buttercream can be frozen (avoid freezing rich buttercream as the yolk may curdle). Do not re-beat chilled buttercream until it has reached room temperature or it could separate out.

DON'T FORGET

If you are filling your cake with buttercream, add a little melted white cooking chocolate to the filling to firm it up slightly and stop it from oozing out.

DON'T FORGET

If a white buttercream is needed, a white vegetable fat such as Trex can be used, but flavouring must be added. A 15 ml spoon of evaporated milk can enhance the taste.

VIDEO LINK

The clip at www. brightredbooks.net/N5PCC shows how to cover a cake in buttercream.

ONLINE

Want to find out more about buttercream? Click on the 'Designer Cakes' link at www. brightredbooks.net/N5PCC

BUTTERCREAM

A very simple **buttercream icing** contains butter and icing sugar. The ratio of sugar is twice that of the fat. This is a soft icing that can be used both as a filler and as a coating for Victoria Sandwiches and Swiss rolls. It is made from unsalted butter and icing sugar. When it dries, it forms an outer crust while remaining soft underneath. If you use a buttery spread, there should be no need to add any additional liquid.

BUTTERCREAM RECIPE

INGREDIENTS
100 g butter
225 g icing sugar
15 ml spoon hot water/milk

METHOD
Beat the butter until light and fluffy.
Sieve the icing sugar onto a plate.
Gradually add the sieved icing sugar, beating constantly, until it is all incorporated.
Adjust the consistency as required by adding a little hot water or milk.

This quantity will be sufficient to fill and coat one 20 cm/8 in cake.

The basic recipe can be adapted. Variations include:

- Almond buttercream – beat in 1 × 5 ml almond essence.
- Chocolate buttercream – beat in 25 g cocoa powder.
- Citrus buttercream – beat in 2 × 5 ml spoons of finely grated lemon, orange or lime rind.
- Coffee buttercream – dissolve 4 × 5 ml instant coffee in 2 × 5 ml boiling water before adding to the mixture.
- Honey buttercream – beat 1 × 15 ml spoon honey into the mixture.
- Rich buttercream – add a fresh egg yolk.
- Vanilla buttercream – use fresh vanilla pods or extract, which has a better flavour than essence.

Buttercream can be coloured. However, it's best to avoid liquid colouring as this can affect the consistency. Use paste colours instead. Avoid adding blue colour as the yellow in the butter can result in green icing.

FROSTING

Frosting is an American term for a cake coating similar to buttercream. It tends to be used to cover the sides and the top of a sponge cake or Swiss Roll. It should have a soft spreading consistency (or may be slightly firmer if required for piping on top of cup cakes), but will have a slightly crisp texture due to the sugar being heated. It cools quickly, so it's important to have the cake ready before you start to make the frosting.

FROSTING RECIPES

INGREDIENTS
175g caster sugar
1 egg white
Pinch of cream of tartar

METHOD
Add the ingredients into a large bowl and place over a pan of barely simmering water. Add 2 × 15ml spoons of water and beat with an electric whisk for approximately 6–8 minutes until soft peaks are formed.
Remove from the heat and use immediately.

This quantity will be sufficient to fill and coat one 20cm/8in cake.

The basic recipe can be adapted. Variations include:

- Caramel frosting – use soft brown sugar instead of caster. Add 2·5ml spoon vanilla essence.
- Chocolate frosting – melt 60g of dark chocolate. Whisk into the frosting once it reaches soft peak stage.
- Vanilla frosting – add a 2·5ml spoon of vanilla essence.

FUDGE ICING

Fudge icing is very similar to buttercream and frosting. However, it involves melting ingredients. It needs to be used quickly, and is suitable for coating a range of sponge, Swiss Roll and Madeira type cakes. It can be spread on with a palette knife or is suitable for piping.

FUDGE ICING RECIPE

INGREDIENTS
25g butter
15ml milk
15ml soft brown sugar
2 × 5ml black treacle
100g icing sugar

METHOD
Gently melt the butter, milk, treacle and soft brown sugar in a small pan.
Remove from the heat and add the icing sugar. Beat until cool.
This quantity will be sufficient to sandwich two cakes together.

The basic recipe can be adapted. Variations include:

- Chocolate fudge icing – melt 25g dark chocolate in the small pan with the other ingredients.
- Coffee fudge icing – 1·25ml spoon of instant coffee can be added to the mixture in the pan.
- Honey fudge icing – add a 5ml spoon of honey.
- Ginger fudge icing – add 1·25ml dried ginger to the mixture. Chopped stem or crystallised ginger can be added to the cooled mixture.

THINGS TO DO AND THINK ABOUT

Looking for a more challenging coating? Why not try to make classic French Crème au Beurre. It is also known as Crème au Beurre Mousseline. It is made with a mousse of sugar syrup and egg yolks, and is a very light, shiny cream which pipes well.

INGREDIENTS	METHOD
150g unsalted butter	Soften the butter in a large bowl. In a second large bowl, beat the two egg yolks.
2 egg yolks	In a small pan, dissolve the sugar in the water then bring it to the boil. You will
50g granulated sugar	need a sugar thermometer to check when it reaches 105°C.
5 × 15ml spoons water	Immediately pour the sugar syrup in a steady stream onto the egg yolks, whisking until thick and mousse-like.
	Whisk this mixture a bit at a time into the softened butter.

FILLINGS AND COATINGS 2

CREAM

Cream is an emulsion of fat in water. It is made from milk. There are different types of cream, and each type contains a different amount of fat.

- Single cream contains 18% fat. It is suitable for pouring; it will not whip.

- Whipping cream contains 35% fat. It can be used for pouring but will also whip to three times its original volume. It is suitable for use as a filling and a topping for light/medium sponge cakes. It can also be piped.

- Double cream contains 48% fat. It is used mostly for whipping and will whip to twice its original volume. It is suitable for piping as well as spreading as a filling/coating.

- Aerosol cream contains 35% fat. It is suitable for use as a topping and for piping; however it must be used quickly as the foam collapses after 20–30 minutes.

- Alternatives to cream – for example, Elmlea – are made of a blend of buttermilk and vegetable oil. They take longer to whisk and may not achieve a peaked result suitable for piping.

Fresh cream is a favourite filling for gateaux and afternoon tea cakes like scones. Double cream has the best flavour due to its increased fat content. You don't have to add sugar to whipped cream, although some recipes might include a small amount of icing sugar and perhaps vanilla extract.

If a cake decorated with fresh cream has to be in a warm room for any period of time, a 5 ml spoon of gelatine dissolved in 10 ml of warm water, cooled then added to the cream will help stabilise the cream.

Flavour can be added to cream once it has been whipped to soft peaks. For example, a small amount of lemon juice, orange juice or liqueur can be added gradually during the final stages of whipping.

CHOCOLATE

Chocolate comes from the seed from the tropical cacao tree. The seeds have an intense, bitter taste so need to be fermented to develop the flavour. The beans are then dried, cleaned, roasted and the shell removed to give cacao nibs. These nibs are ground to a cocoa mass. With the addition of liquid it is known as chocolate liquor. Liquor can be processed into cocoa solids and cocoa butter.

The quantity of fat added to chocolate determines how hard or soft the chocolate is.

TYPES OF CHOCOLATE

Couverture	Has a very high percentage of cocoa butter, which gives it a high gloss. It requires 'tempering' which involves gently heating and cooling the chocolate to stabilise the emulsification of the cocoa solids and butterfat.
Plain (dark)	Can contain anything from 30% to 75% cocoa solids. Opt for a lower percentage of cocoa solids if adding to a cake mixture as the higher the percentage, the more intense the flavour.
Milk	Milk chocolate is plain chocolate with powdered or condensed milk added to it. It is mostly an eating chocolate, but can be used for coating or decoration. Ideally, use milk chocolate with 40% cocoa content. Care must be taken when melting as it is more sensitive to heat than plain chocolate. Milk chocolate contains more sugar than plain chocolate.

contd

White	Strictly speaking, white chocolate isn't chocolate, as it contains no chocolate liquor. It contains cocoa butter, milk and sugar. It imparts a creamy flavour to buttercreams and is useful for decorating. Care must be taken when melting as it does not withstand heat well.
Chocolate flavoured cake covering	This is a blend of sugar, vegetable oil, cocoa and flavourings with only a minimum of 2·5% cocoa solids. It has a higher fat content, which makes it easier to make chocolate curls with. An example of this is Scotbloc.
Cocoa	Cocoa is the powder left after the cocoa butter has been pressed out. The mass is roasted and then ground to make a powder. It provides a good chocolate flavour when baking. Mixing to a paste before using gives the best results.
Drinking chocolate	Drinking chocolate is a mixture of cocoa and sugar. It is usually too sweet for use in cake mixture and lacks depth of flavour.

TEMPERING OR MELTING CHOCOLATE

Tempering chocolate ensures that it has a shine and a crisp 'snap'. Chocolate which has not been tempered tends to be dull, soft and melts easily in your fingers. It's all about controlling the temperature. Chocolate burns very easily if heated above 44°C and can clump into hard, grainy lumps. There isn't much you can do if the chocolate does this, although sometimes adding a little bit of white vegetable fat can help restore it.

There are various ways to melt chocolate:

1 Use direct heat – for example, melt the chocolate in a pan along with a small amount of liquid such as cream. Avoid stirring until the chocolate has melted, and then do so gently.

2 Use a bain-marie, where the chocolate is placed into a bowl above barely simmering water. The bowl must not touch the water: if steam or water get into the chocolate, it can thicken and become a stiff, unusable paste.

3 Use the microwave. Chocolate should be broken into small pieces and checked frequently. Remember that the chocolate will still hold heat once removed from the microwave, so it's better to remove it when it starts to look shiny and stir until smooth.

4 Use the oven. Chocolate can be placed into a shallow dish and heated in the oven for a few minutes at a very low temperature (110°C/Gas mark ¼).

Once melted, chocolate sets best at 18°C or at room temperature. If placed in a fridge, there is a danger the chocolate might develop a white '**bloom**'.

There are two types of chocolate 'bloom' – sugar bloom and fat bloom.

Sugar bloom is usually caused by surface moisture when chocolate has been stored in humid conditions or when it goes from a very cool to a very warm environment. The moisture destroys the sugar in the chocolate, leaving a grainy surface.

Fat bloom occurs if chocolate is not tempered properly or if it has been stored in too warm an environment. Even although the white bloom doesn't look appetising, the chocolate is perfectly safe to eat. Store in a cool, dark place but **not** in the fridge.

DON'T FORGET

The melting point of cocoa butter is just below human body temperature—which is why chocolate literally 'melts in your mouth'.

VIDEO LINK

Watch how to melt chocolate at www.brightredbooks.net/N5PCC

ONLINE TEST

How well have you learned this topic? Take the 'Fillings and coatings 2' test at www.brightredbooks.net/N5PCC

THINGS TO DO AND THINK ABOUT

1 Try piping lines of white chocolate on the top of your chocolate coated cake just before it dries and pull lines with a skewer to give a feathered effect.

2 Want to challenge yourself? Watch The Great British Bake Off master class clip that shows how to make chocolate teacakes (www.brightredbooks.net/N5PCC). Try making your own teacakes.

FILLINGS AND COATINGS 3

It is essential that you maintain a satisfactory standard of personal and kitchen hygiene and safety when carrying out practical activities.

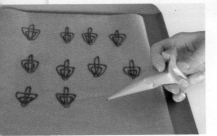

CHOCOLATE (CONTINUED)

USING CHOCOLATE

Grated chocolate – keeping your hands as cool as possible, rub the block of chocolate over the coarse side of the grater in a downwards motion. Make sure you place the grater onto a plate or greaseproof paper.

Dipping food – food can be wholly or partly dipped in chocolate for a decorative effect. Make sure you have a decent depth of chocolate in the bowl (5 cm). A fork or cocktail stick can be used to secure the food to be dipped. When you remove food that has just been dipped, don't rotate it, as this can result in an uneven finish. Shake off the excess chocolate and place the dipped food onto greaseproof paper.

Chocolate leaves – choose undamaged leaves. Clean and dry thoroughly. Brush the underside of the leaf with chocolate. Dry with the chocolate side facing up. Carefully peel away the leaf when set.

Chocolate curls – pour melted chocolate onto a clean, dry surface. A marble slab is ideal. Spread the chocolate with a palette knife until it is smooth and fairly thin. Leave to dry until it is **almost** set. Using a long, thin-bladed knife, hold the knife at an acute angle to the chocolate and pull it towards you with a gentle sawing action. This will scrape off a thin layer which curls into a roll.

Chocolate collar – before you start, place a glass board or marble slab into a freezer. The cake must be prepared and coated with chocolate ganache or buttercream to allow the chocolate collar to stick. Melt the chocolate. Pour onto the frozen board. Spread out with a palette knife. The chocolate will harden very quickly, so as soon as it's spread, score the top and bottom edges to neaten up the collar. Remove with the palette knife, lift and wrap around the cake. The top edge can be adjusted by dipping the palette knife into boiling water and running over the top.

Chocolate transfer sheets – these are sheets of acetate with cocoa butter printed onto them in a variety of patterns. When you spread melted chocolate on these sheets, the cocoa butter pattern is transferred to the surface of the chocolate. Using a spatula, spread the melted chocolate onto the acetate sheet in an even layer and leave to set until the chocolate loses its gloss but remains flexible. This usually takes around 5–10 minutes but can be speeded up by putting the sheet in the fridge. Using cookie cutters or a sharp knife cut out your desired shapes from the chocolate but do not try at this stage to remove your cut-out pieces from the sheet. Allow the chocolate to fully set for a further 20–30 minutes (or place in the fridge for a quicker result). Once set, carefully peel the shapes from your transfer sheet and they are ready to use.

Piping chocolate – once the chocolate has been melted, place into a prepared greaseproof piping bag. (Look out for the link on p55 for advice on how to make a bag.) The chocolate should be a thin, flowing consistency. Very little pressure should be required. Don't over-fill the bag and don't use a piping tube as it is likely to get blocked as the chocolate sets. It is important to hold the bag up off the surface to allow the chocolate to flow and for you to see where you are going to place the chocolate. Designs can be pre-prepared and drawn onto greaseproof paper. Shape outlines can be piped and filled in with different colours.

contd

Chocolate moulds – make sure that the moulds you are using are cleaned and polished. Once the chocolate is melted, pour into the mould. Tap to remove any air bubbles. Leave for a few minutes to settle before tipping out any excess chocolate back into the chocolate bowl. Turn upside down onto greaseproof paper before putting into the fridge.

While the chocolate is cooling, make up the filling. An easy option is to use ready-made **fondant icing** and colour/flavour. Alternatively, you can make up your own. Fondant icing is made from sugar, water and cream of tartar or liquid glucose, which are boiled together until the syrup reaches what is called soft ball stage (when a spoonful of the sugar syrup is dropped into a bowl of cold water and forms a soft ball when rolled between the fingers). The mixture is kneaded into a smooth dough and then colourings or flavours such as peppermint, lemon or coffee can be added.

The filling now needs to be poured into the chocolate shells, so that they are three-quarters filled. Leave these to set. Melt leftover chocolate to fill the top of the moulds. Scrape off any excess and chill. To release, gently tap the mould on the work top. These can be used to decorate a cake or as individual chocolates.

Coating a cake in chocolate – first start with a 'crumb coat'. This involves you adding a thin glaze of ganache or apricot jam to the cake. It gives a better surface for the chocolate to stick to. Melt the chocolate. Place the cake onto a wire rack, over a drip tray or greaseproof paper to catch the drips. Pour the melted chocolate into the middle of the cake and either paddle with a palette knife to gently spread or move the tray to encourage the coating to run down the sides of the cake. Gently tap the wire tray to get rid of any air bubbles and to level the top. Leave to set in a cool place.

GANACHE

Ganache is a glaze or filling made from chocolate and cream. It is used to make truffles.

GANACHE RECIPE

INGREDIENTS
250 g dark chocolate
235 ml double cream

METHOD
1   Place the chocolate into a bowl. Heat the cream in a small saucepan over a medium heat. When the cream has come to the boil, pour it over the chopped chocolate, and whisk until smooth. Stir in flavouring if desired.
2   Allow the ganache to cool slightly before pouring over a cake. Start at the centre of the cake and work outward.

For a fluffy frosting or chocolate filling, allow it to cool until thick, and then whip with a whisk until light and fluffy.

THINGS TO DO AND THINK ABOUT

Undertake some internet research into the range of possible options that you could use to make your own truffles. Select appropriate ingredients and make a range of truffles suitable for a gift.

DON'T FORGET

Brush metallic dusting colours into the mould at the start of the process. These colours work well with dark chocolate.

DON'T FORGET

It is possible to colour chocolate. Melt the required amount of white chocolate before adding paste colour to achieve the desired intensity of colour. Mix thoroughly and use immediately.

DON'T FORGET

If you are using chocolate as a coating, or are using chocolate **sugarpaste** and you get some white icing marks onto it, take a clean brush with some isopropyl alcohol on it and brush to completely remove the marks. The alcohol will evaporate. Never use water.

DON'T FORGET

You can always add flavour/ nuts to your ganache and use this for a centre filling for your chocolates.

VIDEO LINK

Watch how to make ganache and how to ice a cake with ganache at www.brightredbooks.net/N5PCC

VIDEO LINK

Watch the clip on how to make truffles using flavoured ganache at www.brightredbooks.net/N5PCC

DON'T FORGET

If you find your truffle filling is not setting, you can add a knob of butter and stir. It also makes it slightly richer. This mixture will keep for two weeks if refrigerated.

ONLINE TEST

How well have you learned this topic? Take the 'Fillings and coatings 3' test at www.brightredbooks.net/N5PCC

FILLINGS AND COATINGS 4

JAMS

Jam is a set, sweet preserve. To prevent it from being runny, it needs three ingredients to set it: pectin, sugar and acid. Pectin is naturally present in some fruits and is extracted from the cell walls of the fruit by the presence of acid. Fruits rich in pectin include apples, blackcurrants, lemons, cranberries and redcurrants.

Jelly is made by straining the juice from the fruit and discarding the fruit pulp.

Apricot jam is often used for spreading on cakes prior to coating with marzipan. It is preferable to other jams because it has a mild flavour, but any flavour can be used. Coating with jam also prevents crumbs coming off the cake.

Add a little water to the apricot jam, warm it slightly and pass through a sieve to remove any lumps and to make it easier to spread. This also prevents any chunks of fruit sticking to the cake. 200 g is a sufficient quantity to coat the top and sides of one 20 cm/8 in cake. This is usually referred to as 'apricot glaze'.

DON'T FORGET

If you warm the jam in a bowl in the microwave – be careful! It can get extremely hot very quickly.

DON'T FORGET

During hot weather, watch out for leaving an iced cake in a hot room. Jam can ferment under sugarpaste, giving off gases which can cause the icing to bubble up. Try to use fresh jam when possible.

VIDEO LINK

The clip at www. brightredbooks.net/N5PCC shows you how to prepare lemon curd.

DON'T FORGET

If you are not going to use the curd straight away, lay a piece of plastic wrap over the top and press it gently onto the surface before refrigerating to prevent a skin from forming on the top.

CURDS

Most people associate curds with lemon curd. However, curds can be made out of any citrus fruits. They can also be made with puree of berries such as raspberries or blackberries. Curds are not true preserves, but will keep for up to two weeks in a refrigerator.

Because curds contain eggs, cook over a gentle heat while stirring constantly. This will prevent the eggs from cooking too fast and scrambling. Fruit juice is generally high in acidity, so cooking the curd in a nonreactive saucepan or bowl prevents it from developing a metallic flavour. You may need to strain the cooked curd through a sieve to remove any bits of cooked eggs.

MARZIPAN/ALMOND PASTE

Either marzipan or almond paste can be used to cover a Battenberg cake or fill a Simnel cake, but is mostly used as a base layer under fondant/sugarpaste or royal icing, where it helps to trap moisture in the cake. Marzipan is smoother and easier to handle than almond paste. It is made from icing sugar, ground almonds and egg. Two different types of marzipan are available: natural and golden. While they are similar in taste, you are probably best to use natural marzipan under a top coating of fondant icing, because the yellow colour of golden marzipan might shine through.

1 kg of marzipan will be needed to cover a 23 cm (9 in) cake. Prior to use, the marzipan should be kneaded to make it pliable. The work surface can be dusted with icing sugar or cornflour before rolling, but if you add too much, you will dry out the marzipan. Try sprinkling the surface with a little caster sugar instead, or roll out on a non-stick silicone mat.

THINGS TO DO AND THINK ABOUT

1 Apricot jam can be made any time of the year if you use dried fruit. Why not undertake some recipe research and then have a go at making your own batch?

2 Battenberg cake traditionally uses lemon curd as a filling. Develop your own variation on the classic Battenberg cake, still using fruit curd as a filling.

3 After watching the clip on making marzipan fruits, undertake some research into different fruits that you could create using marzipan. Go ahead and make them. Get a classmate to evaluate the finished items in terms of their overall realistic appearance (including shape, design proportion, texture and colour balance).

DON'T FORGET

Do not overwork marzipan by kneading for too long, or the oil will be released from the almonds and it will become greasy.

DON'T FORGET

When it's warm weather, be careful not to store an iced cake in a hot room as the marzipan can ferment if it has come into contact with flour.

TOP TIP

Marzipan is best worked at room temperature. Any marzipan that is not being used should be stored in a plastic bag to prevent it drying out.

TOP TIP

If your marzipan gets a little dry, and starts to crack, knead in a little bit of white fat to make it more supple.

TOP TIP

Marzipan can be frozen. For best results, cut into small pieces and wrap tightly in several layers of cling film before freezing. Remember to thaw completely before using, and definitely don't defrost in the microwave!

TOP TIP

You can colour marzipan very effectively with paste colours.

TOP TIP

For a great tasting chocolate marzipan, mix together equal amounts of marzipan and chocolate modelling paste.

VIDEO LINK

Watch the clip on how to make marzipan fruits at www.brightredbooks.net/N5PCC

ONLINE TEST

How well have you learned this topic? Take the 'Fillings and coatings 4' test at www.brightredbooks.net/N5PCC

FILLINGS AND COATINGS 5

TOP TIP

It is important that all the equipment you use to make your royal icing is grease free, as any grease present will make the icing heavy.

TOP TIP

Royal icing should be mixed at the slowest speed if you are using an electric mixer. It is better to beat it by hand as you will feel the texture change, but it does take longer.

TOP TIP

Royal icing is at its strongest the day it is made. The older the icing, the weaker it becomes, so try not to prepare it too far in advance. Ideally, store it for a maximum of seven days.

TOP TIP

While you are in the process of using royal icing, always store it at room temperature and cover it with a damp cloth. Never store it in a plastic container. If you want to keep it and use it later, place a piece of cling film onto the icing surface to exclude any air, as air will make the icing dry.

TOP TIP

If your icing has been sitting for more than a couple of hours, it must always be re-beaten by hand to bring it back to peak before using.

TOP TIP

Royal icing can be coloured. Liquid colouring is the most suitable as you can count the number of drops you add, allowing you to mix up a similar batch if you have to make more up.

ROYAL ICING

Royal icing is used for celebration cakes, such as wedding cakes, because when it sets it is strong enough to support tiers of cake. It is not applied directly to a cake because it would lift crumbs and discolour the icing.

There are three options when making royal icing:

USE FRESH EGG WHITE

Often a few drops of blue food colouring are added to counteract the off white colour caused by using fresh egg. A little lemon juice helps to strengthen the albumen in the fresh egg but be careful not to add too much as it can cause the icing to break during piping. Although the high sugar content in the icing probably means it will not support bacterial growth, you are probably best, for food safety reasons, not to make your own royal icing using fresh (uncooked) egg white in school.

USE DRIED ALBUMEN

Meri White is a popular brand of dried egg white and it has brightener and stabilizers added. You dissolve the powder in water and use it straight away.

INGREDIENTS
60 ml warm water
15 ml dried albumen
450 g icing sugar

METHOD
Place the warm water into a bowl.
Add the dried egg white, mix and leave for 10 minutes.
Gradually beat in the icing sugar, but not all at once as this will produce a dull, heavy icing. The icing is ready when it is light and slightly glossy in texture and should be capable of forming a peak.

This quantity will be sufficient to cover one 20 cm/8 in cake.

USE A PACKET MIX

Literally, the product is placed in a large bowl, water is added and it is mixed until the desired consistency is reached. Again, it is better to add all the icing gradually and mix, not beat.

Glycerine is normally added to royal icing to stop the icing drying out fully, so that the cake can be cut with a knife and doesn't require a hammer and chisel! Glycerine should only be added once the icing has been beaten to **firm peak**. The normal ratio is 5 ml glycerine for every 2.2 kg of icing sugar. Do not add glycerine if the cake is to hold tiers.

SUGARPASTE

Sugarpaste is also known as fondant icing, or ready-to-roll icing. It is a soft, pliable paste that is used to cover cakes such as Madeira, Sultana and Rich Fruit cake. It colours easily so is often used for novelty cakes.

INGREDIENTS
500 g icing sugar
1 egg white
2 x 15 ml liquid glucose

METHOD
Put the egg white and liquid glucose into a large bowl.
Beat in the icing sugar until the mixture becomes stiff.
Lightly dust the work surface with some icing sugar.
Knead the paste until smooth and pliable.

This quantity will be sufficient to cover one
20 cm/8 in cake.

Ready-coloured sugarpaste can be purchased. However, if you are colouring it yourself, remember to add the colour a little bit at a time. Doing small batches at a time, then kneading the pieces all together, is a more manageable way to colour large amounts. Paste colours are best, as liquid colours will make the paste too sticky. When left, the colours develop and usually deepen. Sometimes spots of colour appear, so it's always a good idea to knead the paste thoroughly before use. If you add too much colour, add in some white colour paste.

THINGS TO DO AND THINK ABOUT

Follow the link at www.brightredbooks.net/N5PCC to get some top tips for working with sugarpaste. Why not make a poster giving your own top tips for working with sugarpaste, or any of the other fillings and coatings mentioned in this unit.

VIDEO LINK

Watch the clip at www. brightredbooks.net/N5PCC to find out how to colour sugarpaste.

TOP TIP

Rubbing white fat onto your hands before adding colour to sugarpaste will act as a barrier and stop food colour from staining your hands. Alternatively, wear disposable gloves.

TOP TIP

To store sugarpaste, wrap it in cling film, then place it in a plastic bag (to prevent any air getting to the paste and drying it out) and, finally, put it into an airtight container. Do not store in a refrigerator as it can lose its elasticity and become difficult to work with. Home-made paste will keep for up to one week, and shop bought for 1–2 months.

TOP TIP

If you have frozen the paste, it must be thoroughly defrosted before use. If it feels a little stiff when you start to use it, rub a little white fat onto your hands and knead the paste well.

ONLINE

Not sure how much sugarpaste you will need to cover the size of cake you have made?
Click on the link at www. brightredbooks.net/N5PCC to find out.

ONLINE TEST

How well have you learned this topic? Take the 'Fillings and coatings 5' test at www. brightredbooks.net/N5PCC

TOOLS AND THEIR USES 1

If you use the right tools for the job, it will make cake decorating quicker and easier, and will help you to achieve more professional results. Some specialist equipment might have to be sourced from specialist shops or the internet. But be warned! Once you start to see the vast range of equipment that is available, and what you can do with it, you'll soon need a bigger tool box to hold all your new purchases!

CAKE STAND/TURNTABLE

This allows your cake to be elevated from the work surface, making it more convenient to reach and decorate. A large upturned bowl can be used to do a similar job.

SMOOTHER

A **smoother** can be used to erase rolling pin marks on fondant icing and ensure that it is polished to give a smooth, professional finish prior to decorating. Slightly cupping your hand and gently smoothing the iced cake can give similar results, but make sure all rings are removed first.

ROLLING PIN

When it is used for decorating purposes, a small, non-stick silicone pin is ideal. It is used to roll out small amounts of modelling paste.

There is also a huge range of **textured rolling pins** that just need to be rolled over the icing to give an instant patterned effect.

A roll-and-cut **silicone mat** with a non-stick surface is a good way to gauge the size of icing you need to roll out, as the sizes are marked on the mat. The non-stick surface can also help prevent the icing sticking and reduce the need to add cornflour onto the surface, which can dry out the icing.

When you are rolling out **flower paste**, a small **work board** is a good idea. The best option is to choose one that is flat on one side and has grooves cut into the other side, along with different sized holes. You can use the grooves for leaf veining, and use the holes when forming flowers or leaves that start off with Mexican hats.

You can also buy **CelPads** (also known as foam pads) with holes in them to form Mexican hats. You can use these pads to hold previously cut out shapes in place so you can thin, frill or soften their edges. If you have cool hands, you can actually place the flower paste shape onto your upturned hand and use the fleshy part below your thumb to do the same job. But be warned! If you have hot hands, you'll get better results with a foam pad!

KNIVES

A **serrated knife** has jagged edges. It allows you to cut into a cake without damaging it and creating lots of crumbs. Ideally, you are looking for a long blade that covers the whole diameter of the cake.

A **palette knife** is used to spread icing onto a cake. Its flexibility allows you to lift small pieces of decoration up and onto a cake. Some palette knives have a raised handle and they come in all shapes and sizes to manage a range of different tasks.

> **TOP TIP**
>
> It's a good idea to rub your board lightly with some white fat before rolling your paste out to prevent it from sticking.

> **TOP TIP**
>
> To shape or carve a sponge or Madeira cake, it is a lot easier if the cake is frozen or chilled prior to cutting.

contd

A **small**, **sharp craft knife/scalpel** is perfect for all types of craft work, whether cutting out designs in paper or sugarpaste, as the blade is fine and sharp and does not snag or pull the paste. It is an ideal tool to pick out bits of modelling paste that might have got stuck in cutters that you are using.

PIPING BAGS

Piping bags come in a variety of sizes and can either be washable or disposable.

The reusable bags are usually made from cotton and sometimes have a plastic interior coating, which helps protect the buttercream from staining the material with colour/flavour. The coating also stops the buttercream from oozing through the seams. Try to steer clear of the thin nylon type, as these are far too flimsy and your hands will become very greasy when using them. Also, their seams are prone to bursting while you are piping.

Disposable plastic piping bags are often bought in rolls of 100 and, although cheaper to buy than washable bags, they obviously have to be thrown away after use. They do, however, save time and are very convenient to use.

You can also get **duo piping bags**, which allow you to pipe two different colours at the same time.

They can be used with different nozzles (sometimes called tubes) to create decorative borders, lettering and all sorts of other details, including flowers.

For better control, the ideal option is to make your own bag out of greaseproof paper. Make up a batch before you start to do any decorating.

NOZZLES AND COUPLERS

Nozzles/tubes fit onto piping bags using a two-piece coupler with a threading mechanism. This holds the nozzle in place securely and allows you to change the nozzles without too much fuss. The base of the coupler sits inside the bag, while the outer part holds the nozzle in place and screws onto the base. You could, of course, just pop a nozzle into a disposable bag without the need to use a coupler, but you would not be able to change the nozzle without using a new bag.

Nozzles range from fine writing tubes [size 0 or 1] to large tubes that will allow you to create stars, petals, basket weaves, scrolls and other exciting shapes.

PAINTBRUSHES

The sizes of paintbrushes vary and textures range from soft to hard, but no cake decorating box should be without at least two or three paintbrushes. They are used to paint on colour, dust finished pieces with dusting powder, brush melted chocolate into moulds and paint on fine detail when making sugarpaste models.

A fine sable brush is ideal for painting details such as features on faces. The lower the number, the finer the brush. 0 or 00 is ideal. A flat brush is better for dusting on colour.

THINGS TO DO AND THINK ABOUT

Make a poster that gives clear instructions – ideally with drawings – about how to make a piping bag out of greaseproof paper. Use your instructions to practise making up your own bags.

DON'T FORGET

The blades on a scalpel are extremely sharp, so always keep covered when not using. Also, wash and dry thoroughly to avoid the risk of any rust on the blade.

VIDEO LINK

Watch the clip that shows you how to make a disposable piping bag out of greaseproof paper at www.brightredbooks.net/N5PCC

ONLINE

Visit the Digital Zone to find out more about the different sizes and types of nozzles and what you could do with them.

DON'T FORGET

Usually, the smaller the nozzle, the thinner the icing should be. Also, the work should be finer so it is better to use a smaller piping bag to give you more control.

DON'T FORGET

To clean confectioner's varnish off your brush, immerse in isopropyl alcohol immediately after use. If you don't do this, the brush will be wasted and you will need to throw it out.

ONLINE TEST

How well have you learned this topic? Take the 'Tools and their uses 1' test at www.brightredbooks.net/N5PCC

TOOLS AND THEIR USES 2

CRIMPERS

These tools are used to pinch together the edges of soft icing to give a decorative effect. They look a little like a large set of tweezers. Crimpers come with a black ring, like an elastic band, around them. It's really important to keep this on the **crimper** as it creates a steady tension and, therefore, a uniform effect. They come in a range of sizes and decorative effects – for example, serrated scallop, heart shape, diamond or wavy line.

If you opt to do crimping as a finishing technique on your final cake, there will be a possible five marks available to you for doing the following:

- Choosing the correct equipment and preparing it for use. (You should check the equipment is clean. You might also need to put a little bit of cornflour on the edges of the crimpers to prevent them from sticking to the soft icing.)
- Using the crimping tool correctly. (Don't forget the purpose of the black band, and never be too heavy-handed or else you could cut into the marzipan or even the cake below the icing.)
- Positioning the tool in relation to your design.
- Carrying out the crimping it before the icing hardens.
- Being accurate with the spacing and sequencing of your crimped pattern.

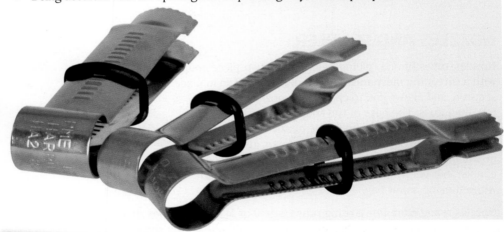

EMBOSSING TOOLS

Embossing is a decorative technique where a design is pressed into soft sugarpaste.

You can use special embossing tools such as a teddy bear shape. You can also use an embossing mat, which will give a **texturing effect,** such as a brickwork or tree bark effect, or you could just use buttons, jewellery, the tops of icing nozzles or any other clean item that will leave a shape when pressed into the icing. It is really important that embossing takes place before the icing hardens.

If you use embossing as a finishing technique on a final assessment cake, you will get marks for the following:

- Choosing and using the correct equipment.
- Using the embossing tool correctly – that is, not being either too heavy-handed or too light-handed, but pressing it in to show the design and its outline clearly.
- Following your design idea and making sure that any pattern is spaced appropriately.

MODELLING TOOLS

There is a vast range of modelling tools that allow you to shape, frill, hollow out or add detail when modelling with paste or marzipan. The main tools that you would probably use most often include the following.

BALL TOOL

This has a large ball on one end and a smaller ball on the other. It is ideal for making round holes – for example, for marking out teddy bear feet. It can also be used to frill edges of shapes cut from flower paste and it's great for rounding centres of flowers/leaves.

BONE TOOL

This is similar to the ball tool. It can be used to make holes and frill edges, and is particularly good at forming eye sockets or arm sockets.

CELL STICK

These come in all different sizes and thicknesses. The pointed end is useful for opening up centres of flowers. They are particularly good at frilling petals made from flower paste. However, a cocktail stick could be used as a cheaper alternative.

DRESDEN TOOL

This is a most useful tool for fluting and frilling petals. It will help to increase the size of any petal. Its pointed tip is used to emphasise the centre of some flowers while the veining end allows you to easily create a veined effect on flowers and leaves.

SCALLOP AND COMB TOOL

This is sometimes called the 'smiley face' tool: it is often used to press a quick and easy smile into a sugarpaste-modelled face. The comb side is excellent for creating textured lines. It is also ideal for creating a 'stitched' effect when modelling teddy bears.

CONE TOOL

This tool is useful for making sockets. It can also give a lovely star pattern, which is, particularly useful if you are aiming to achieve a quilted effect.

BLADE AND SHELL TOOL

This is a useful tool, as both sides are used for very different purposes. The shell part is great for making a pattern on the edge of a board or on the top edge of a cake. It is also a simple way of marking out animals' paws. You can use the blade end without worrying about using a sharp knife. The point can be used to make dots, or even to remove pieces of unwanted paste from a patchwork cutter.

VIDEO LINK

If you want to see video tutorials on a whole range of tools, click on the 'Designer Cakes' link at www. brightredbooks.net/N5PCC You can register to access a whole range of free tutorials.

ONLINE TEST

How well have you learned this topic? Take the 'Tools and their uses 2' test at www.brightredbooks.net/ N5PCC

THINGS TO DO AND THINK ABOUT

Take time to practise using the different tools on a board covered with sugarpaste, or on a dummy cake covered in paste.

TOOLS AND THEIR USES 3

VIDEO LINK

Watch the clip to see how to use plunger leaf cutters to make some holly leaves at www.brightredbooks.net/N5PCC

ONLINE

Find out more about using cutters by following the link at www.brightredbooks.net/N5PCC

TOP TIP

To look after your metal cutters, wash and dry them as normal, then place them into an oven that has been heated to 50°C for 10 minutes to dry them out thoroughly and prevent rust forming.

TOP TIP

When you are using a cutter, a little white fat rubbed onto the inside edge of the cutter will help the paste to slide off smoothly.

VIDEO LINK

The clip at www.brightredbooks.net/N5PCC shows you how to use a patchwork cutter to make and decorate a butterfly.

DON'T FORGET

Dust your mould with a little cornflour before you add the paste to prevent it from sticking.

TOP TIP

Lustre colour can be brushed into moulds instead of cornflour to help release the shape and create a dusting of colour.

CUTTERS

These are used to cut out flower and leaf shapes, as well as a whole range of other options such as letters, hearts, circles, people and animals. They come in different sizes and are available in metal and plastic.

Metal cutters tend to give a neat edge, but if they are not looked after properly they can rust. You are best to use plastic cutters with a circular motion on a CelPad/foam pad to give a professional finish.

Using a cutter is a quick and easy way to produce required shapes. It also gives you identical and uniform shapes each time, which is important when you are decorating to a set pattern. But don't forget that you can also be creative with other pieces of equipment if you don't have the right cutter. For example, you could use the wide end of a piping nozzle to give a small circle shape.

You can also buy plunger cutters. These not only cut out the shape you are looking for – they will also give you an embossed/veined effect when you press them down, thereby saving you time and giving an excellent finish.

PATCHWORK CUTTERS

Before rolling out your paste, spread some white fat onto the board. It's best to use flower or **Mexican paste**, and it needs to be rolled until it's thin, but not too thin. (Use the depth of the cutter as a guide.) Try to avoid picking the paste up off the board as you want it to stick down. Rub your cutter with a little bit of white fat, before pressing it into the paste. Press firmly. To remove the cutter, find an edge and try to put your nail underneath so that you can flick it off – pulling off the cutter tends to pull the paste, which isn't what you want. Panic not if the cutter flies across the room when you flick it!

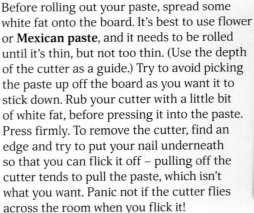

MOULDS

There are three main types of moulds available:

1 **Plastic** moulds are made from thin sheets of plastic that have been moulded. These are mostly used for chocolate work.

2 **Hard resin** moulds are excellent when you are trying to prevent distortion – for example, when you are moulding faces.

3 **Silicone** moulds are now the most widely available moulds. They are extremely easy and quick to use, and easy to care for.

contd

Moulds are very simple to use, provided you select the correct paste and it is of the right consistency for the particular mould you have chosen. The secret of success for many moulds is to use a firm paste such as flower or Mexican paste, but don't be afraid to experiment and use other pastes such as marzipan and fondant (with a little added **gum tragacanth** for strength) or modelling chocolate.

Possibly one of the most useful moulds you can buy is one that allows you to mould incredibly realistic hands. Watch Frances McNaughton demonstrate it on her website: http://www.franklysweet.co.uk/videos.php#

WIRE

When making wired flowers it's best to use cotton-covered wire. You can buy these in different gauges. The thickness of the wire is given as a number. Softer wire has a higher gauge number and is used for small, delicate flowers (for example, No. 33), whereas thicker wire has a lower gauge number and is used for heavier, larger flowers (for example, No. 24). If you are making a heavier flower and don't have the right gauge of wire, you can tape a few wires together to give additional strength.

FLORIST'S TAPE

Florist's tape is made from paper that contains its own glue. It comes in different colours and might need to be cut to half or quarter its original width. The tape should be wound down the wire stem at an angle, starting at the top and overlapping the edges, pulling slightly as you twist to encourage it to stick. Its job is to strengthen or colour wire or to secure different wired pieces together into a spray.

VIDEO LINK

Karen Davies is an experienced cake decorator who regularly uses moulds in her cake designs. Go to www.brightredbooks.net/N5PCC for a range of clips that show her using moulds to produce a variety of effects. Using a mould is an ideal way to get detail when modelling.

VIDEO LINK

Want to make a face? Watch the clip at www.brightredbooks.net/N5PCC

DON'T FORGET

Wires should never be inserted directly into a cake. A posy pick can be used. Check the glossary for more information on posy picks.

VIDEO LINK

Watch how to cover wire with tape at www.brightredbooks.net/N5PCC

ONLINE TEST

How well have you learned this topic? Take the 'Tools and their uses 3' test at www.brightredbooks.net/N5PCC

THINGS TO DO AND THINK ABOUT

1 Experiment with taping any wired flowers you have made with different colours of tape. Which do you prefer? Why?

2 Experiment with making a range of different faces from sugarpaste/modelling paste. Try adapting the shape. Add different features such as hair, teeth, glasses, freckles. Work on the detail that turns your face into a real character.

TOOLS AND THEIR USES 4

FOOD COLOURING

There are a lot of different food colourings now available. Here's a quick guide to the different types on offer.

PASTE COLOURS

These are thick and concentrated. They are ideal for colouring sugarpaste and flower paste. Add a little bit at a time, using a cocktail stick, and knead into the paste to get the colour you want. Remember, the colour will dry a little darker. Some people wear latex gloves to protect their hands when using colouring paste. If you need an intense colour – for example, black as opposed to grey – go for a paste labelled as 'extra'.

POWDER DUSTS

The simplest way to use these dusts is to apply them with a brush. They can be mixed with white spirit (alcohol) for painting on sugarpaste. Alternatively, you can mix them with confectioner's varnish for painting. This makes the powder stick better once dry, whereas the alcohol will just evaporate and the colour could rub off. Lustre dusts tend to give a brighter, more metallic finish.

LIQUID COLOUR

This is useful for colouring royal icing or buttercream, but it's not a good idea to use it with sugarpaste because it can be very messy and it makes the paste consistency a bit too sticky.

SPRAY COLOUR

There is a specialist piece of equipment called an airbrush that enables you to create sprayed colour effects, but a cheaper alternative is to use ready-to-use lustre spray from a can. This gives your cakes a real shimmer. Take care not to get too close to the surface you are spraying and be very careful because the spray colour will go everywhere! It's a good idea to place your cake into a spray booth you have created with a cardboard box.

contd

GLITTER DUSTS

These will certainly give a sparkly effect, but be careful because many of them are classed as 'non-toxic, non-edible'. They are not harmful and if eaten, they will just pass through your system. However, the advice from the Food Standards Agency is **not** to eat them and to include glitters only on items that will be removed before the cake is eaten.

SUGAR ART PENS

These are edible pens that are perfect for writing on sugarpaste or for adding facial features. Just make sure the lid is kept on the pen when not in use as it will dry out.

EDIBLE GLUE

This is also known as sugar glue. It is used to stick together pieces of dry icing, or to add a model that has already been coated in sugarpaste onto a cake. You can use water instead of glue if both items are still fresh and soft.

You can buy pots of **edible glue**, but you can also make your own by taking a small piece of sugarpaste, adding water to it and mixing it to a sticky mixture.

FINALLY...

A metal sieve is good for pushing sugarpaste through to create strands of hair or a beard. A garlic crusher is great at doing the same thing. Use the same technique with yellow paste to create a realistic-looking centre of a daisy.

A pasta machine is a great way to create uniformly thin sheets of paste.

THINGS TO DO AND THINK ABOUT

Why not try making your own edible glitter? Here's how:

1 Preheat the oven to 250°C.

2 Put a quarter of a cup of water in a small pan.

3 Dissolve 2 x 15 ml spoons of gum Arabic in the water by heating gently over a low heat. Do not allow it to boil.

4 When dissolved, pass it through a small strainer. Liquid colour can be added at this stage if you wish.

5 Cover a baking tray with foil. Spread the mixture onto the tray and bake in the oven until it is dry and flaky.

6 Remove from the oven and brush off from the tray onto greaseproof paper.

7 Sandwich between two sheets of paper and squash with a rolling pin. Store in an airtight jar.

DON'T FORGET

You can mix dusting colours with white fat to make a paste that can be used to add colour onto an embossing tool.

VIDEO LINK

For an in-depth tutorial on all the different types of dusts and how to use them, click on the link at www.brightredbooks.net/N5PCC

TOP TIP

Use a 1·25 ml spoon of CMC powder mixed with 30 ml of cooled boiled water to create your own sugar glue. Add both to a small jar, shake and leave in the fridge overnight before using. You can add a few drops of white vinegar as this will act as a preservative and allow the glue to last for a few weeks.

DON'T FORGET

You only need to brush a thin coat of glue to the surface. Leave it for a few moments to become tacky before adding the item to be attached.

ONLINE TEST

How well have you learned this topic? Take the 'Tools and their uses 4' test at www.brightredbooks.net/N5PCC

FINISHING APPLICATION TECHNIQUES 1

In this unit, you are asked to demonstrate your ability to apply a range of finishing techniques to cakes and other baked items. The techniques that you will be required to undertake include:

- Trimming
- Rolling
- Smoothing
- Spreading
- Coating
- Piping

Assessment for this unit will involve you selecting and preparing appropriate fillings and coatings, depending upon your chosen cake or baked item. You will need to have a plan that you can follow when carrying out the finishing and you must work at all times in a safe and hygienic manner. You will need to carry out this activity independently, under controlled conditions, while being supervised by the person assessing you. You may be asked to complete a workbook as evidence that you have successfully met the required standards.

DON'T FORGET

Never attempt to carve a freshly baked cake, as it will be too crumbly. Ideally, leave the cake to rest for a minimum of 12 hours before splitting/cutting/filling.

TOP TIP

As with shaping a cake, it is easier to take away than to add on when trimming the bottom edge of a cake, so trim off a little at a time before smoothing.

DON'T FORGET

Buttercream that has just been removed from the fridge is extremely difficult to spread, so make sure it is at room temperature before you use it.

ONLINE

Learn more about icing a cake in buttercream by following the link at www.brightredbooks.net/N5PCC

TRIMMING

You are required to use appropriate equipment to trim or shape the baked item. This will usually be a small sharp or serrated knife, although you could also use a revolving cutter/pastry wheel. The key to success is to cut off a little at a time, until you have the required shape. If you do cut off more than you need, don't panic – you can stick the cake back on with a little buttercream – but take care not to do this too often as it might make the sugarpaste slip when you come to coat the cake. Ideally, trimming should be minimal so that the size and shape of the cake remains acceptable.

Using a firm, moist cake such as Madeira that can be cut and shaped without crumbling gives the best chance of success. Carving a cake that has just been removed from the freezer also helps prevent the cake crumbling too much.

Be prepared in advance before you even bake your cake. Think carefully about the tin you are going to use to bake your cake. Choose one that's the closest in shape to what you are trying to achieve. Always have a picture or drawing of what you want to achieve in front of you as you carve the cake

You also need to demonstrate your ability to trim the base effectively after coating a cake. In this case you should consider the following:

- Use the correct equipment – for example, a small, sharp knife.
- Achieve a smooth edge with no gaps and no ragged edges.
- Keep wastage to a minimum.

You can also use a smoothing tool to trim the bottom edge of a cake that has been coated in sugarpaste. Hold the smoother at a 45° angle, press down and pull the excess paste away. This might need a bit of practice, but once mastered, will give an excellent result.

SPREADING

No matter whether you are spreading jam, buttercream or royal icing, you should aim to follow these guidelines:

- Use the correct equipment for spreading – for example, a palette knife.
- Prepare the medium to be spread correctly, and ensure it is of the appropriate consistency – for example, soft peak for royal icing and light and aerated for buttercream.
- Ensure that there is an even coverage of the medium.

It is a good idea to place the cake onto a cake board and then onto a turntable. This makes it easier for you to turn the cake around as you spread the coating, so that you can get an even coverage. Remember, an upturned bowl does the same job if you don't have a turntable.

ROLLING

No matter whether you are rolling marzipan or sugarpaste, you should aim to follow these guidelines:

- Prepare the product you are planning to use by first kneading it until it is soft and pliable. This will get rid of any cracks.
- Use appropriate equipment/utensils – usually a rolling pin. A large, non-stick pin is ideal.
- Roll the product to an appropriate size, shape and thickness. Try placing wooden strips (chop sticks are ideal for this job) on either side of your paste – this will ensure that it is rolled to a uniform thickness (ideally 5mm).

Dust the work surface with a little bit of icing sugar. If you are using marzipan, try dusting the surface with caster sugar, which will not dry the paste out. Rolling out on a non-stick mat can also reduce the amount of icing sugar you need to use on the surface.

Remember to place the wooden strips on either side of your paste before you begin. Roll the paste out a little in one direction. Rotate by 90° and roll a little more, aiming to keep the paste in a more or less circular shape. As the circle becomes larger and thinner, pick up the paste using the rolling pin rather than your hands, as this prevents the paste stretching. Keep rotating the paste and rolling a little more until the rolling pin runs smoothly over the wooden strips. You should now have a circle of paste of even thickness that is ready to cover your cake.

To prevent tearing the product as you lift it, carefully roll it over the rolling pin, then move it across onto the top of the cake. Unroll and smooth over the top and sides. If you have an air bubble in your sugarpaste, pop it as soon as you see it by inserting a sterilised pin at 45° and stroking out the air, then continue to roll.

THINGS TO DO AND THINK ABOUT

Experiment with different methods for rolling out sugarpaste and marzipan. Try the following:

1 Roll out on a work surface dusted with (a) icing sugar (b) cornflour (c) caster sugar.
2 Roll out on a silicone mat without any additional dusting.
3 Roll out between sheets of greaseproof paper.

Evaluate your results. Which method do you think gave you the best result? Why do you think this is the case?

TOP TIP

When rolling, start with your fingertips on the rolling pin and roll all the way along onto the palm of your hands and over your wrists if your paste is large enough. If you just use your fingers to roll, you will get ridge marks on the paste.

TOP TIP

Remove unwanted air bubbles in sugarpaste by popping them with a sterilised pin.

DON'T FORGET

If you have had to pierce an air bubble and it has left a visible hole, wait until the sugarpaste is dry and then add a little royal icing the same colour as the sugarpaste to plug up the hole. Wipe away any excess before smoothing.

DON'T FORGET

Avoid using cornflour to roll out marzipan as it will cause fermentation.

ONLINE TEST

How well have you learned this topic? Take the 'Finishing application techniques 1' test at www.brightredbooks.net/N5PCC

FINISHING APPLICATION TECHNIQUES 2

VIDEO LINK

There are lots of different ways to coat a cake. The clip at www.brightredbooks.net/N5PCC shows one way of coating a rich fruit cake in marzipan.

VIDEO LINK

The clip at www.brightredbooks.net/N5PCC shows how to cover a cake in royal icing.

VIDEO LINK

If you have coated your cake, and perhaps spot an air bubble or a mark on it, watch the clip at www.brightredbooks.net/N5PCC to see how to sort out some common problems.

DON'T FORGET

Remove any excess icing when it is wet as it's much harder to remove when dry.

TOP TIP

You can coat a cake board in royal icing in two different ways. The quickest and easiest method is to leave the board until you have finished coating the sides of the cake then, while the icing is still wet, coat the board with soft icing and smooth with a palette knife. The alternative is to coat the board separately, giving it three coats, like the cake itself, for a superior finish.

TOP TIP

Do not leave the board to dry in a warm place, or the icing will dry shiny like a run-out instead of matt like the cake coating.

COATING

Types of cake coatings suitable for a sponge cake include: chocolate, marzipan, sugarpaste, royal icing, buttercream and frosting. If a cake has had a first coating of marzipan, you could add sugarpaste or royal icing as a top coating. You can create an adhesive surface on the marzipan by brushing it with cooled, boiled water, using a pastry brush. This allows the sugarpaste to stick to it.

When coating a cake, think about the following:

- Use the appropriate equipment/utensils.
- Prepare the product to be used as a coat correctly.
- Apply adhesive if required before coating – for example, buttercream.
- Make sure the cake base is covered appropriately.

You can also show your skills in coating by covering a cake board (or drum) in sugarpaste.

COATING A CAKE IN ROYAL ICING

To achieve the correct consistency of royal icing for coating a cake, add half a teaspoon of glycerine to each 500 g of icing. This will make it easier to cut once the cake is coated.

For the first coat of icing, make sure it has reached full peak to achieve a good covering. Place the icing in the centre of the cake and paddle outwards towards the edge. Paddling with a palette knife not only spreads the icing, but also removes some of the air bubbles. Use a long knife or a ruler and pull the blade evenly across the cake. A scraper and turntable are useful tools to use when coating the sides of the cake. Leave it to dry before adding a further two coats.

SMOOTHING

When smoothing, the following points should be followed:

- Use the correct equipment – for example, a cake smoother.

- Achieve a smooth finish with no cracks and no fingerprints or marks.

- Use a smoothing tool to smooth out any imperfections or air pockets, without adding any finger marks. Ideally, use two smoothers: one to rest on the top of the cake and the other to smooth the sides.

Don't worry if you don't have a smoothing tool – your hands can do a similar job. However, always remember to remove any jewellery and dust your hands lightly with icing sugar to prevent sticking.

Another option is to use a ball of the spare sugarpaste you have trimmed off the cake as a smoother. Just remember to dust it lightly with icing sugar to prevent it from sticking.

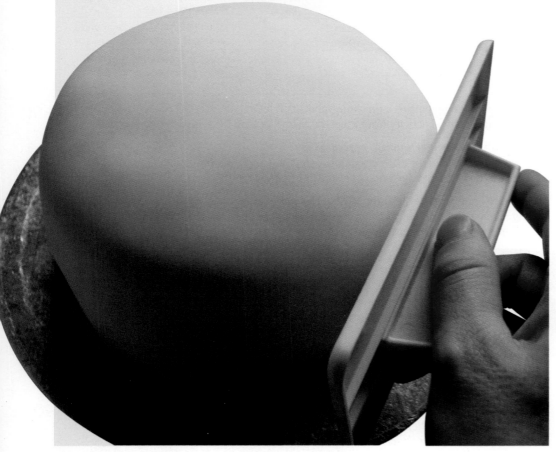

THINGS TO DO AND THINK ABOUT

Produce an illustrated help sheet that shows the steps to follow when coating a rich fruit cake in marzipan. You could also do your own YouTube clip of you preparing and coating the cake.

TOP TIP

When preparing your sugarpaste, you have to knead it. The purpose of kneading is to add heat, which will help to smooth out the cracks in the paste before you use it. Knead in a similar way to bread dough, but watch out for over-working the paste, and don't add extra icing sugar as this will just dry the paste out.

ONLINE

Head to www.brightredbooks.net/N5PCC and check out the handy leaflet which gives you some great hints and tips on to how to cover a cake with sugarpaste.

VIDEO LINK

Watch the clip at www.brightredbooks.net/N5PCC to see a cake being covered in sugarpaste.

TOP TIP

Roll out your sugarpaste and give it a good rub over with your hands or with a smoothing tool to polish the surface before you coat your cake. This will help get rid of any unwanted icing sugar and remove any air bubbles.

ONLINE

The short clip at www.brightredbooks.net/N5PCC demonstrates how to cover a board in paste. It also demonstrates a new technique for trimming the paste using a smoother instead of a sharp knife.

DON'T FORGET

You should always choose a cake board/drum that is approximately 3 in/7·5 cm bigger than your cake. To give a decent depth of icing, use 500 g for a 12 in/30·5 cm board/drum.

ONLINE TEST

How well have you learned this topic? Take the 'Finishing application techniques 2' test at www.brightredbooks.net/N5PCC

FINISHING APPLICATION TECHNIQUES 3

PIPING

Royal icing can be piped directly onto a cake coated with sugarpaste or royal icing, or it can be piped onto greaseproof paper or acetate and then attached to the cake. The possibilities are endless. However, you must first make sure that you get the consistency of the icing right.

A quick guide to the consistency of royal icing required for different decoration techniques

CONSISTENCY	DESCRIPTION	USE
Thin icing	Finds its own level in the bowl when gently tapped	Run-outs and flooding
Soft peak	Forms a soft peak when the spoon is lifted out and the peaks stand up but droop over at the tip	Embroidery work and fine writing First coat on a cake
Medium peak	Firmer peak that holds its shape	Most piping patterns – for example, **snail trail**, stars
Firm peak	Peaks stand firmly without dropping over at their tips and will not fall when shaken	Petals for flowers and large shell patterns that need to hold their shape

When undertaking piping as a finishing application technique, you will probably be observed during your practical activity. Your assessor will be looking for evidence that you have:

- used the equipment/utensils appropriately
- prepared the icing or other medium correctly
- achieved even coverage and consistency of piping.

It is really important not to have any air bubbles in your icing. Stir it carefully before using. Once you have placed the icing into a piping bag, wrap the bag in plastic and then in a damp cloth to prevent it drying out when you are not using it.

To start piping, place the nozzle you are going to use into the bag. Fill the bag only two-thirds full. Overfilling just means you run the risk of icing squeezing out of the top of the bag, wasting icing and making a mess. Fold the bag down, forcing the icing down and expelling any air. To hold the bag, turn your hand so that the palm faces up. Place the bag in between your index and middle fingers, with your thumb on top. The pressure squeezing the icing should come from your thumb.

LINEWORK

To pipe a line, touch the nozzle against the surface where you want to start your line. Start squeezing. Once the icing starts to flow, slowly lift the piping bag up. Creating sufficient distance between the nozzle and the surface will allow you to see where you are placing your line. The key to success in piping is to maintain even pressure. If you squeeze too hard, your line will go curly and if you don't squeeze hard enough, your line will fade and break.

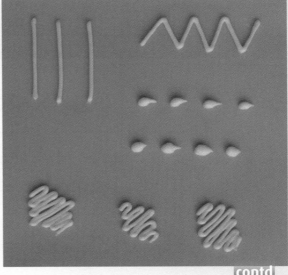

contd

As well as straight lines, you can pipe zig-zags, lettering and so on. You can also use a fine tube to produce teardrops.

Trellis work is produced when you pipe a set of parallel lines. Let them dry before piping another set of parallel lines across the first set.

Overpiping is when a second line of piping is piped on top of the existing line, making the outline stand out more. A smaller nozzle number is used to pipe the second line. For example, a number 1 nozzle is used to pipe on top of the original line, which has been piped from a number 2 nozzle. The first line must be left to dry before adding anything on top.

Another basic linework technique is to use a plain tube to pipe **bulbs**. Hold the bag at a 90° angle. Squeeze with an even pressure to form a bulb of icing. Gently release the pressure. If you get a little peak forming on top, use a damp paintbrush to dab it down. You can produce different effects on a cake, or as a border, using different sizes of bulbs.

A very effective way of providing edging decoration is to do something called a '**snail trail**'. Use a plain nozzle or, alternatively, just snip the bottom of a greaseproof bag. Hold your piping bag at a 60° angle. Squeeze to make a bulb of icing, release the pressure and pull the icing forward to make a tail. Squeeze again to make another teardrop of icing, and another, and another. Again, you can vary the size of your 'snail trail' by squeezing out smaller or larger bulbs of icing.

A very simple, but effective, technique is to pipe a **star**. You can use a large or small star tube. Hold the piping bag vertically and squeeze out the icing. Stop pressing the bag to stop the flow of icing and lift up to form a point to the star. Stars can be piped into a border or a large area on the top, or the sides of a cake can be covered in stars.

Still using the star nozzle, hold the bag at a 45° angle and squeeze to give a bulb of icing. Stop squeezing and pull the bag forward to form a tail. Squeeze again to form the next shell shape. Continue to do this to form a **shell border**.

The star nozzle can also be used to pipe rosettes, scrolls and twisted rope patterns.

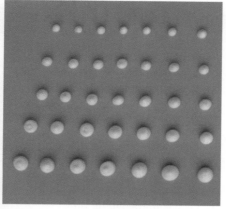

bulbs

snail trail

stars, shell border and rosettes

 ## THINGS TO DO AND THINK ABOUT

Practise your piping techniques. Put together a set of labelled photographs with an instruction guide so that you can refer back to it each time you undertake piping as a decorative technique.

FINISHING APPLICATION TECHNIQUES 4

TOP TIP

You can make three dimensional **filigree** shapes by carefully piecing together dried filigree shapes. In this instance, you will get more stability in your shape if the squiggly lines touch slightly.

TOP TIP

Highlight the brush strokes by dusting with lustre dust.

VIDEO LINK

Brush embroidery can also be done using softened sugarpaste. Watch the tutorial at www.brightredbooks.net/N5PCC to see how it's done.

PIPING (CONTINUED)

CORNELLI OR FILIGREE

This technique can be used to cover areas of a cake. You can pipe directly onto a cake or you can pipe onto non-stick paper. Use a fine piping tube (number 1 is ideal) and pipe a continual line of random W and M shapes.

If piping onto paper, keep the lines close together and leave to dry for 24 hours before removing from the paper with a palette knife.

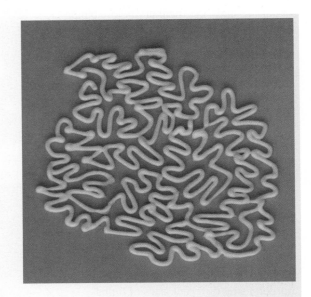

BRUSH EMBROIDERY

Embroidery is another piping technique that can be used to provide a decorative effect on a cake. It can be piped directly onto a cake or can be piped onto an iced plaque, which is then placed onto the cake.

Start with embossing your design onto the icing. Leave this to dry. Use a number 2 or 3 nozzle to pipe over the outline of the shape. Pipe an additional line of icing inside the outline. It is this second line of icing that you will drag to create the effect. Work a small area at a time so that the icing doesn't dry out.

Use a small, damp paintbrush to brush the icing from the outline into the centre of the shape. Texture can be created by adding extra-fine piped lines or by brushing another layer over the first one once it has dried.

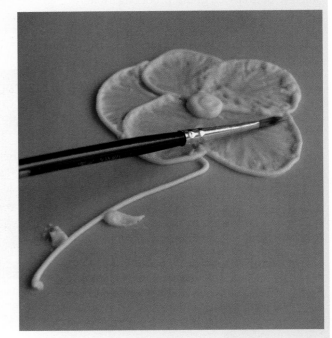

RUN-OUTS

Before you attempt a run-out, you will need non-stick paper or acetate, plus an outline of the shape you want to produce.

Run-outs are made by piping an outline and then filling in the outline with thinner icing. This technique is sometimes known as **flooding**. To be successful, it is really important to use fresh royal icing, but be careful when you are beating it as this could add air

contd

bubbles you don't want. To test that you have the correct consistency, pull a knife across the icing surface; the mark should disappear by the time you count to ten. Once you have traced your design onto paper, secure it to a flat surface and pipe over the outline with firm peak icing. Leave this to dry.

To fill in the outline, you don't need to use a nozzle – just cut a small hole at the bottom of the bag. Hold the point close to the outline and squeeze out the icing. You can use a paintbrush to get the flooded icing close to the piped outline. Don't attempt to do the whole area at the one time.

When the run-out is complete, leave it to dry in a warm room. It could take between 24 and 48 hours before you should attempt to peel the design off the paper.

COMMON FAULTS

Here are some common faults to avoid when icing a cake:

- The icing appears porous – if you over-beat royal icing it dries to a crunchy, almost foamy texture.

- The icing appears sticky once piped – it could be that you have added too much colour, or that some oil has got into your icing and has affected the texture.

- The icing is hard to get out of the bag – it will probably be too dry – add some extra water to it.

- The line you are piping keeps breaking – it could be that you aren't applying enough pressure.

- You've got a blob of icing at the start of your line of icing – it could be because you aren't pulling the icing away quickly enough. If the blob forms at the end of your line, it could be because you haven't released the pressure quickly enough.

- The shape you have piped hasn't kept its definition – it could be that your icing is too thin.

THINGS TO DO AND THINK ABOUT

For extension work on piping, watch Elaine MacGregor as she shows you how to scribe a design onto a cake, and then do lace extension and intricate piping work at www.brightredbooks.net/N5PCC

FINISHING DECORATION TECHNIQUES 1

The Cake Finishing unit aims to develop a range of specialist skills and creative techniques, including colouring, piping, modelling, stencilling, crimping, embossing, texturing and the use of commercial cutters/aids. These techniques should be applied to cakes and other baked items with creativity, flair and resourcefulness, using appropriate tools and equipment.

MATERIALS: AN OVERVIEW

There are lots of different types of materials you can use for modelling and creating finishing designs. Some are edible and others are non-edible. This section of the book will explain some of these materials and describe which is best for which technique. Try experimenting with as many of them as possible. In time, you will start to develop a preference for the type of paste you like to work with.

SUGARPASTE

Sugarpaste can be used to coat a cake, but can also be used to make a wide range of models. It cannot be rolled as thin as some of the other pastes, so it won't give such a delicate finish to things like flowers.

Most people opt to buy sugarpaste instead of making it. It is available from a wide range of outlets and in lots of colours. If you do want to try making your own sugarpaste (also called rolled fondant icing), try the following recipe:

SUGARPASTE RECIPE

1   Put 1 egg white and 2 × 15 ml of liquid glucose into a bowl.

2   Beat in 500 g of icing sugar bit by bit, until the mixture becomes stiff.

3   Tip the mixture out of the bowl onto a work surface dusted with icing sugar, and knead the paste until it is soft and pliable.

MODELLING PASTE

Modelling paste is sugarpaste with CMC or gum tragacanth added and is mostly used to make models. The addition of the CMC/gum makes the sugarpaste firm but pliable so it is easy to work with, and it also allows the models to dry harder and keep their shape. There are lots of ready-made modelling pastes on the market, including pre-coloured pastes.

If you want to model in chocolate, you could try making your own chocolate modelling paste using the following recipe:

CHOCOLATE MODELLING PASTE RECIPE

1   Melt 125 g of chocolate over a pan of hot water.

2   Once melted, remove from the heat and stir in 2 × 15 ml spoons of liquid glucose.

3   Put the paste into a plastic bag and chill for an hour until firm, but pliable.

It can be stored for several weeks.

TOP TIP ⬆

A natural gum called gum tragacanth is widely used to make modelling paste, but there is a man-made alternative known as carboxy methyl cellulose (CMC) which is cheaper than gum tragacanth. It also goes further, so will last you longer. Thicken sugarpaste to make modelling paste by adding 2·5 ml of CMC powder per 250 g of sugarpaste.

TOP TIP ⬆

If you need to colour modelling paste, it is better to add the colour to the sugarpaste before adding the CNC/gum tracaganth, because sugarpaste is easier to knead than modelling paste and will give you a more even colour.

DON'T FORGET ➕

If you find that your models aren't holding their shape, just knead some extra CMC/gum tracaganth into the paste.

MEXICAN PASTE

Mexican paste is much stronger than modelling paste due to its greater gum tragacanth content. It is an ultra-fine modelling paste which is ideal for plaques, frills, drapes and cards. You can also use it with moulds and patchwork cutters. It is less stretchy than flower paste. It sets firm, but remains soft enough to eat.

MEXICAN PASTE RECIPE

1   Mix together 225 g of icing sugar and 3 × 5 ml level teaspoons of gum tragacanth.

2   Add 6 × 5 ml of cold water.

3   Knead well.

4   Store in a plastic bag overnight (not in the fridge).

5   Knead small pieces until pliable before using.

The paste can be used straight away or frozen for later use.

FLOWER PASTE

Flower paste (sometimes called gum paste or petal paste) is a firm, sweet paste that is mostly used for modelling flowers. It also works well when used with moulds. You must be careful to work with small amounts at one time and to store any unused paste in a plastic bag, as it will get spoiled if exposed to air. It dries firm and is delicate, so be careful not to drop your flowers as they will shatter into pieces.

Flower paste is very strong, which means it can be rolled out very thinly without tearing. This makes it ideal for delicate flowers and leaves. It is edible, but because it dries so hard, it is brittle to the touch and is mostly used for items placed onto a cake that would be saved, not eaten. Flower paste tends to be more expensive than other pastes, but you don't need to use much, so a pack can last between 6–12 months as long as it is stored correctly.

FLOWER PASTE RECIPE

1   Mix 2 teaspoons of gelatine with 5 teaspoons of water in a bowl. Place over a pan of hot water and stir until dissolved.

2   Add 2 teaspoons of liquid glucose and 3 teaspoons of white fat and continue to stir over heat until combined.

3   Sieve 500 g of icing sugar and 3 teaspoons of gum tragacanth into a bowl.

4   Add 1 egg white and the gelatine mixture to the icing sugar and beat with an electric whisk on low speed to combine. Increase the speed and beat for 5–10 minutes until it becomes white and stringy.

5   The paste should be placed into a plastic bag and then an airtight box before being placed into the fridge for 24 hours before using it.

Flower paste can be purchased in a range of colours. You can also colour your own. Paste and powder colouring both give good results. When making dark-coloured flowers, it is best not to colour the paste too deeply; when the item is dry you can dust all over with a deep-coloured dusting powder.

 DON'T FORGET

Flowers made from flower paste must be stored in a cardboard box, and not in a plastic box, because plastic will make the flowers sweat and droop.

 ONLINE TEST

How well have you learned this topic? Take the 'Finishing decoration techniques 1' test at www.brightredbooks.net/N5PCC

 THINGS TO DO AND THINK ABOUT

Experiment with making the same item – for example, a rose – with a range of different types of pastes. Evaluate your results. Which paste did you prefer working with? Why? Which rose looks best? Why do you think this is the case?

FINISHING DECORATION TECHNIQUES 2

PASTILLAGE

Pastillage is an alternative to flower paste. It can be used for modelling and for making plaques. It can be made and used immediately. To make your own pastillage, try the following recipe:

1. Sprinkle 7·5 ml of powdered gelatine onto 4 × 15 ml of water in a bowl and leave to soften.

2. Sift 2·5 ml of gum tragacanth and 500 g icing sugar into a bowl and warm gently over a pan of hot water.

3. Warm the gelatine mixture over hot water and stir to dissolve.

4. Add the gelatine to the sugar mixture and beat on a low speed with an electric mixer for about 3 minutes.

It can be refrigerated in an airtight container.

As pastillage dries bone hard, its normal use is for decorative ribbons, appliqués and 3D shapes. Pastillage is made from 100 per cent edible ingredients, but it's not advisable to eat it because it would probably break your teeth! It is, however, useful for creating key structures that need to be strong – for example, a box or a length of tree bark on which you can lay some flowers.

Pastillage cannot be rolled as thin as flower paste and, when you are using it, you have to work quickly because it dries very fast.

ONLINE

Find out more by checking out the Artista Soft website link at www.brightredbooks.net/N5PCC

VIDEO LINK

Watch a rose being made from Artista Soft in the clip at www.brightredbooks.net/N5PCC

ARTISTA SOFT

Artista Soft is an opaque, non-toxic, non-edible, air-drying modelling paste. Its main ingredients are potato flour and rice flour. It is extremely light to use and contains its own glue, so it will not stick to your hands. It is virtually unbreakable when dry. It dries with a cloth-like finish that is as light as a feather. It works well with cutters, veiners and moulds. You can buy it in white and colour dust as required, or you can buy a range of bright colours.

Be careful to keep any unused paste tightly sealed: it is air-drying and will, therefore, harden if not stored correctly. Although, working with Artista Soft feels totally different to working with flower paste, it is an excellent medium for modelling once you get used to it. It is especially good for making delicate shapes like flowers, because they won't break if dropped.

ONLINE

Find out more about SugarVeil at www.brightredbooks.net/N5PCC

VIDEO LINK

Watch how to make SugarVeil lace at www.brightredbooks.net/N5PCC

SUGARVEIL

SugarVeil is a powder that you mix with boiling water to form a decorative icing. It is similar to royal icing in that you can use it to pipe on or off a cake, but when it is set, it can be cut or peeled off greaseproof paper.

Once it is made up, SugarVeil can be spread onto a lace mat. When it's dry, it can be peeled off to give amazing effects. It can be coloured, and flavour can also be added.

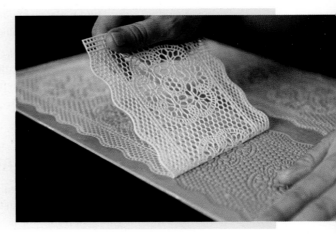

COLD PORCELAIN

Cold porcelain is a non-edible, air-drying paste made from cornflour, glue and baby oil. It can be used in exactly the same way as flower paste but must **not** be placed directly onto a cake. One major advantage of using cold porcelain to model flowers is that it is much stronger and will not break if dropped.

You can buy ready-made cold porcelain paste, but you can also make your own fairly easily. Why not try the following recipe?

COLD PORCELAIN RECIPE

INGREDIENTS
125 g cornflour
2·5 tablespoons of baby oil
115 ml craft glue
115 ml white PVA wood glue
Few drops white oil paint

METHOD
Place the baby oil into an old saucepan along with the two lots of glue. Stir in the cornflour. Don't panic if the mixture is slightly lumpy at this stage.
Place the pan over a medium heat and stir until the paste comes away from the sides of the pan and forms a ball. This should take approximately 10 minutes.
Remove the paste from the pan onto a non-stick board and knead. If the paste is very sticky, return to the pan and cook for a bit longer. Overcooked paste is difficult to work with.
Wrap in plastic and leave to cool. Re-knead and place into another plastic bag and then into an airtight container.
Before you use the paste, squeeze in a little white oil paint. This helps to prevent it drying a greyish colour.

Handling cold porcelain is very similar to handling flower paste. Use cornflour to prevent sticking and use glue to stick flowers together. It's worth noting that the paste shrinks a little as it dries.

 ONLINE

Step-by-step instructions on how to make cold porcelain can be found at www.brightredbooks.net/N5PCC

 THINGS TO DO AND THINK ABOUT

1   Develop a handy guide to modelling materials. Include the pros and cons for each type of paste.

2   Use pastillage to make a set of place cards. You can decorate them in any way you like. Try using a range of techniques – for example, crimp the edges or emboss with a patterned rolling pin. Use royal icing to pipe names on the place cards. You could dust or paint over the names.

ONLINE TEST

How well have you learned this topic? Take the 'Finishing decoration techniques 2' test at www.brightredbooks.net/N5PCC

FINISHING DECORATION TECHNIQUES 3

To achieve a pass in the Cake Finishing unit, you will be required to apply at least two finishing decoration techniques to a baked item. By doing so, you should achieve an aesthetically pleasing overall effect.

COLOURING

VIDEO LINK

Watch the clip at www. brightredbooks.net/N5PCC on how to colour sugarpaste.

You should use the following criteria to colour your decorating medium successfully:

- Prepare the medium correctly – for example, knead sugarpaste until soft and smooth.
- Apply the colouring correctly – for example, use a cocktail stick and add a small amount of colour at a time.
- Knead to achieve an even consistency of colour on a work surface dusted lightly with a little icing sugar.

You can check the colour is evenly distributed by cutting the sugarpaste in half. Remember, a little colour can go a long way, so add a tiny bit of colour at a time.

MARBLING

This is achieved by partially blending two colours of sugarpaste together to create a streaked effect. Be careful not to over-knead as the more you mix, the less obvious the **marbling** effect will be.

SPONGING

You can give your cake, or covered cake board, a mottled effect by using a sponge and some food colouring. Dilute liquid food colouring with some clear alcohol. Dip the sponge into this mixture to dampen it (make sure it isn't too wet) and then dab it onto the icing. Make sure it is totally dry before you add a second colour.

STIPPLING

Stippling food colour onto paste is a simple and effective method of adding colour. Use a medium-sized firm bristle paintbrush and only add a little of the diluted colouring onto the tip of the brush. Blot off excess onto kitchen paper before repeatedly dotting the brush over the surface of the paste. Keep the paintbrush vertical.

PAINTING

To add detail, you can paint directly onto a cake or paint features onto a model you have made. Mix paste or powder colour with a little clear alcohol and use a very fine brush. Blot excess liquid from your brush on absorbent kitchen paper. Make sure each layer of colour is dry before painting on another colour. If you make a mistake, don't panic. Adjustments can be made using a clean paintbrush or cotton bud dipped in clear alcohol to remove the painted mistake.

VIDEO LINK

The clip at www. brightredbooks.net/N5PCC shows how you can paint directly onto an embossed design on a cake.

ADDING PATTERN TO YOUR PASTE

Be creative with paste colours. Here's an idea to try:

1 Roll three strips of coloured paste and three strips of white – all the same size.

2   Lay the coloured strip on top of the white strip and roll up. Do this with all three pieces. Cut into slices.

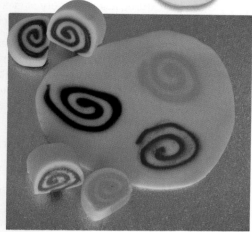

3   Roll out the white sugarpaste to cover your cake. Add the coloured spirals on top and roll to incorporate in a pattern of your choice.

You can use the same idea to create candy-striped lines in your paste. To create that effect, stack a series of long rectangular pieces of paste. Slice vertically to form candy stripes which you can then roll into the paste.

DON'T FORGET

If you plan to colour your paste to an intense colour, it is a good idea to wear plastic gloves as the food colouring can stain your hands. Alternatively, rub your hands with a little white fat as this will act as a barrier.

TOP TIP

To make natural looking, flesh-coloured paste, mix together white paste with a little peach colour.

CRIMPING

Crimping is a decorative effect that you can produce on the top edge of a cake, at the base of the cake or on the iced cake board. A crimping tool is like a big set of oversized tweezers that you press together to create the effect. They come in all sorts of different sizes and styles. Crimping is carried out on soft sugarpaste.

To be successful at crimping, remember the following:

- The black rubber band around the crimper allows you to adjust the width of your pattern.
- Crimp while the fondant icing is soft.
- Practise on a spare piece of fondant first to check your spacing and sequencing.
- Dip your crimper into some icing sugar before you start to prevent it from sticking.
- Enhance your crimping patterns with lustre dusts or piping.

VIDEO LINK

Watch the guide to crimping at www.brightredbooks.net/N5PCC

VIDEO LINK

The clip at www.brightredbooks.net/N5PCC shows how to crimp a board covered in sugarpaste.

EMBOSSING

Lightly grease the embossing tool with some white fat to prevent sticking.

- Always emboss soft sugarpaste prior to it hardening.
- Apply just enough even pressure to leave an even, visible print mark on the icing. Press too hard and you will cut into the icing.
- When embossing in a pattern, ensure that your spacing is accurate and your indentations are to the same depth each time.
- The design can be enhanced by painting, dusting or adding some royal icing piped effects.

VIDEO LINK

Check out the 'Patchwork Cutters' clip at www.brightredbooks.net/N5PCC

VIDEO LINK

The clip at www.brightredbooks.net/N5PCC will show you how to paint an embossed design.

ONLINE TEST

How well have you learned this topic? Take the 'Finishing decoration techniques 3' test at www.brightredbooks.net/N5PCC

THINGS TO DO AND THINK ABOUT

Undertake some research to find out where your closest cake decorating supplier is.

FINISHING DECORATION TECHNIQUES 4

VIDEO LINK

The clip at www.
brightredbooks.net/N5PCC
shows you how easy it is to
use a texturing mat to give
sugarpaste a design effect.

TEXTURING

Surfaces can be textured using a variety of everyday materials such as a new scouring pad, toothbrush, fine grater or sponge, as well as specialist **texturing** mats and embossers.

- The surface should be textured before the sugarpaste hardens.
- If you are using a mat, roll over the top using even pressure. Spraying with lustre spray or dusting with powder can enhance the effect.
- If you are texturing by hand, make sure you achieve accurate spacing and sequencing. It's a good idea to plan ahead here with an accurate drawing showing exactly where you plan to place the effects.

Other effects that you could consider as a background include:

GRASS

- You could cover the cake board/cake with green sugarpaste and stipple with a sponge dipped in green royal icing.
- You could use a metal sieve to push green coloured sugarpaste through to form tufts that look like grass.
- You could colour desiccated coconut with green liquid colour and leave to dry or toss in some powdered green dust colour.
- You could pipe green coloured royal icing using a specialist nozzle (No. 233).

SAND

- Colour caster sugar, or semolina, orange/brown with paste colouring and allow to dry.
- Use Demerara sugar – lightly dampen the surface of the cake or board and sprinkle the sugar on top for a sand effect.

SNOW

- For a very simple snow effect, dust heavily with icing sugar.
- Sprinkle some white magic sparkles onto soft sugarpaste or fresh royal icing.
- Royal icing can be peaked up with a fork to create a snow effect.

MODELLING FIGURES

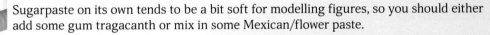

Sugarpaste on its own tends to be a bit soft for modelling figures, so you should either add some gum tragacanth or mix in some Mexican/flower paste.

Once you master the basic shapes required for figure modelling, you can then start to create different facial expressions and add clothing and other details to personalise your models.

If you opt to undertake modelling on your final practical activity, you will be assessed on your ability to do the following:

- Select and prepare appropriate equipment and materials correctly.
- Create a correctly proportioned and shaped model.
- Use a suitable adhesive in an appropriate manner.

Extra credit will be given for appropriate finishing details such as facial features.

BODY

The key to success is getting the different body parts in proportion. Aim to make the head a quarter of the size of the body.

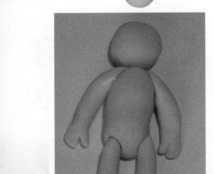

To form the body, roll the paste into a ball. Use your little finger to roll across the ball to form the waist. A bone or ball tool can be used to form arm and leg sockets.

Make both legs at the same time to ensure they are the same size.

HEAD

A head is simple to make; you just need to roll a smooth ball of paste. You can model your head by hand, or you can use one of the moulds available for this purpose.

To model a head and face by hand, start with a smooth ball of paste. Add eyes, a nose and ears. Use your modelling tools to help add features. Eyebrows and hair can be painted on or hair can be added by pushing some brown sugarpaste through a sieve. Alternatively, it can be piped on with coloured royal icing. You can give your head some extra character by adding teeth, freckles, dimples, a frown or even a hat.

ARMS AND HANDS

When making arms for a figure, they should start right at the top of the shoulder and come to about halfway down the thigh. The easiest way to create arms is by rolling a sausage of paste and cutting it diagonally in the centre. If you want to insert a hand, use your ball tool to make a hole at the bottom end, and insert a hand into this sleeve space. Alternatively, you can form a hand by cutting fingers or using a hand mould.

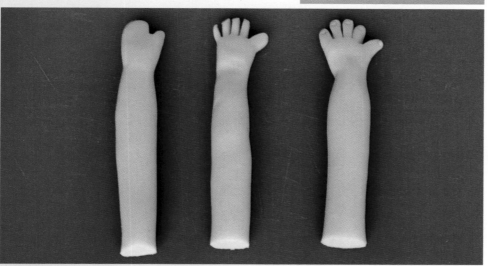

TOP TIP

If you are uncertain about the proportion of your models, you can use a paste size guide.

TOP TIP

When making a free-standing model, place it onto a small non-stick board while you are making it to allow you to move the piece around without handling it.

TOP TIP

Spread a thin layer of white fat onto the palm of your hand when rolling small sausages of paste. This will stop the paste from crumbling and allow you to roll extremely thin pieces.

VIDEO LINK

Watch Carol Deacon creating a very simple sugarpaste figure, a simple sugarpaste face and hair for the model at www.brightredbooks.net/N5PCC

TOP TIP

Instead of using spaghetti or a cocktail stick to support a modelled figure, make an edible version by using some leftover Mexican paste and roll into a long, thin sausage shape. Cut into different lengths and leave to dry for at least 6 hours.

ONLINE TEST

How well have you learned this topic? Take the 'Finishing decoration techniques 4' test at www.brightredbooks.net/N5PCC

 ## THINGS TO DO AND THINK ABOUT

Do some research into Scottish cake decorators. Create a collage of their work to display.

FINISHING DECORATION TECHNIQUES 5

DON'T FORGET

Check out pages 66-9 in the Finishing Application Techniques section of the book for information and advice on piping.

VIDEO LINK

Watch the tutorial on using a stencil at www.brightredbooks.net/N5PCC

VIDEO LINK

The clip at www.brightredbooks.net/N5PCC shows a range of cut-out shapes being used to decorate a cake.

TOP TIP

When you are making a rose and you have moulded the paste onto hooked wire, check the cone is the correct size by measuring it against the 5 petal cutter – ideally it should fit within a single petal shape.

STENCILLING

Stencilling requires a steady hand. You need to hold the **stencil** firmly against the cake. Apply the icing or colour evenly and be extremely careful about lifting the stencil away without smudging the design. If you do smudge the colour or royal icing, don't panic – use a fine paintbrush dipped in alcohol to remove the error.

To be successful at stencilling, remember the following:

- Use the correct equipment.
- Stencil onto dry/set sugarpaste.
- Ensure a neat finish with no runs or smudges.

USE OF COMMERCIAL CUTTERS/AIDS

Cutters come in all shapes and sizes – for example, heart, snowflake, leaf and flower petals. You need to think carefully about the medium you are going to cut to ensure it is appropriate for the purpose intended. For example, if you want to cut out a leaf and include it as part of a spray of flowers as a cake topping, you would use flower or Mexican paste. If you want to cut out a heart for the top of an iced cupcake, you could use sugarpaste.

Plunge cutters are also available. Some of these have a **veiner**, which makes realistic-looking leaves quickly and easily.

- Make sure that the medium you plan to use has been worked well and rolled out to the appropriate thickness.
- The cutter might need to be lightly greased with white vegetable fat or dusted with icing sugar/cornflour before using to prevent it from sticking.

You could use water to attach a freshly-cut sugarpaste item onto a recently covered cake. Alternatively, you could use a spot of royal icing or edible glue. Remember you can add water to sugarpaste and mix it down into a sticky glue like paste.

SUGAR FLOWERS

One of the simplest flowers you can make is a blossom filler flower. It can be used to fill out a spray or posy. Here's how you make one:

- Roll out a small piece of flower paste thinly.
- Cut out flowers with a **blossom cutter**.
- Thread a **stamen** through each flower and secure by piping on a dot of royal icing.
- Tape the flower onto fine gauge wire.

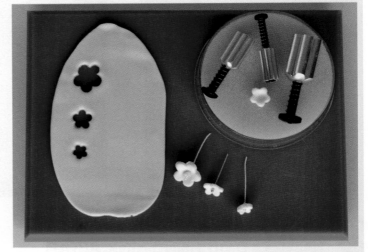

Different effects can be created by inserting coloured stamens, changing the size of the cutter and by colouring the petals in different ways.

contd

CALYX

Sugar flowers are often finished off by adding a **calyx**. To make a calyx, start by rolling a ball of green paste into a cone. Pinch and roll out to form a hat shape. Place the calyx cutter over the top and cut out. You can thin out the calyx shape by using a ball tool and you can make fine cuts to give a more natural appearance.

LEAVES

There are many varieties of leaf cutters available. To make a leaf, roll out a ball of green flower paste. Cut out using the required leaf cutter. Wire can be inserted if you leave a thicker ridge down the centre of the leaf or you can roll some flower paste onto the wire. Press the leaf into a veiner firmly, using a little edible glue to ensure that the wire sticks to the leaf. This can then be left to dry before being dusted with a mixture of colours (moss-green and aubergine give a realistic rose leaf effect).

To steam leaves, boil the kettle and wave them through the steam vapour, but be careful not to scald yourself! Be sure to ask your teacher for help when trying this.

THINGS TO DO AND THINK ABOUT

Take a photograph of one of the cakes you have produced and are most proud of. Write an article to explain the ideas behind it. Send both to a cake decorating magazine or a school publication.

DON'T FORGET

It is a good idea when making a dark-coloured leaf to add dusting colour to the paste and then over-dust with the same colour once it is dry: this will give a more uniform colour.

TOP TIP

Once you have dusted leaves with colour, steam them before painting them with confectioner's varnish. This stops the colour coming off the leaf and it means that only one coat of varnish is required.

VIDEO LINK

There are lots of different clips available online about how to make sugar flowers. The clip at www.brightredbooks.net/N5PCC provides a basic introduction to making flowers.

DON'T FORGET

There are some excellent cake decorating books on the market. If you want to develop your skills in making sugar flowers, Mary Ford's book *Decorative Sugar Flowers for Cakes* is an excellent guide (ISBN 1-85479-405-1).

ONLINE TEST

How well have you learned this topic? Take the 'Finishing decoration techniques 5' test at www.brightredbooks.net/N5PCC

FINISHING DECORATION TECHNIQUES 6

TOP TIP

Use greaseproof paper and measure out and mark slits at regular intervals. Use this to cut the slits into the sugarpaste on the cake to ensure even spacing.

TOP TIP

Use royal icing to pipe a decorative effect along the line where the scalpel has made the cuts to neaten the finish.

VIDEO LINK

The clip at www. brightredbooks.net/N5PCC shows how to carry out ribbon insertion.

TOP TIP

If you want to attach a ribbon round a cake, you should use good quality satin ribbon. Place the ribbon into water and then pull it through your fingers to remove excess moisture. Place the ribbon around the cake, making sure there is a slight overlap at the back. You can then secure it by using double-sided tape. Do not use a pin as this is not safe.

TOP TIP

If you plan to use the inlay technique directly on a covered cake, it's important that you don't brush the marzipan with water, as you need to be able to remove the section(s) without them sticking to the cake.

ADDITIONAL TECHNIQUES

RIBBON INSERTION

To produce this effect, freshly coated sugarpaste is cut at regular intervals, and small lengths of ribbon are inserted into the slits to look like the ribbon has been threaded through the icing. Given the potential hazard caused by using ribbon, an alternative option is to thinly roll out paste (a ratio of half sugarpaste to half flower paste would be good). Cut the paste into strips and insert these into the prepared slits. If you have access to one, using a ribbon cutter keeps the strips parallel and neat, and is very simple to use.

You could also use a strip of paste instead of ribbon, as discussed above and produce a completely edible cake. This also gives you the option of adding a crimped and/or an embossed design, which not only makes the cake look more attractive but is a great way of showing extra skills in a final cake.

INLAY

This easy technique involves cutting out a section of (sugarpaste) icing and replacing it –usually with a different colour – to create an effect.

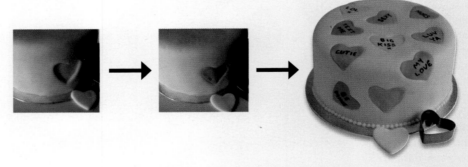

An alternative option is not to replace the section cut out and to leave it as an effect. This works particularly well if the cake has been coated initially with chocolate paste, then topped with white sugarpaste. Why not try cutting out circles then adding a stitching effect around the edges of the holes?

APPLIQUE AND BAS-RELIEF

These are techniques where you use a cutter or template to produce a shape. With applique, additional shapes (usually in different colours) can be cut out and placed onto the original shape to build up the design. With **bas-relief**, after cutting out the original shape, you use small pieces of sugarpaste to build up areas of the design, before cutting out the same shape as the base and adding to the top.

contd

GARRET FRILL

This is a decorative frill made from flower or Mexican paste. Sugarpaste alone isn't suitable for a **garret frill** as it is too soft and tends to stretch, but you could use a ratio of half sugarpaste to half flower paste. It is usually applied around the side of a cake or can decorate the edge of a plaque.

Here's how to make a garret frill:

1 Lightly mark a line on the cake where you want to place the frill.

2 Roll out the paste thinly. Cut out the frill using a garrett frill cutter (or you can use a ordinary fluted cutter and use a plain cutter to cut out the centre).

3 Cut through the circle to make one long frill. Place onto a CelPad and use a cel stick or cocktail stick to frill the fluted end.

4 Dampen either the edge of the frill or the cake itself before placing it onto the cake. If you want to, you can add another layer on top.

5 You could add some colour by dusting the bottom of the frill. Another option is to pipe along the top edge or roll along a quilting wheel to give a stitched effect.

 VIDEO LINK

Want to see exactly how to create a garret frill on a cake? The clip at www.brightredbooks.net/N5PCC will show you how.

PHOTO CAKES

Want to add a personalised photo onto a cake? Companies such as Deco (http://deco.uk.com/) sell icing sheets that can go through a printer. Check out their website for more information.

 ONLINE TEST

How well have you learned this topic? Take the 'Finishing decoration techniques 6' test at www.brightredbooks.net/N5PCC

 ## THINGS TO DO AND THINK ABOUT

1 Make a spider diagram of all the possible decoration techniques you could use on your baked items.

2 You have been asked to deliver a cake decorating demonstration. The session should last 30 minutes. Plan what key skills you would like to show before delivering your demo to your classmates.

COURSE ASSESSMENT

PRACTICAL ACTIVITY

The National 5 Practical Cake Craft course has one component that makes up the final assessment:

- Practical activity worth 100 marks.

The practical activity requires you to use the skills you have learned throughout the course to bake and finish a cake according to a given design brief. The marks you get contribute 100% of the overall marks for the course assessment. The course will be graded A–D. The practical activity will be done under supervised conditions.

The key skills, knowledge and understanding the practical activity will assess include:

- Your ability to bake a cake and execute finishing decorations.
- Your ability to use specialist tools and equipment with flair and dexterity.
- Your ability to demonstrate creativity and resourcefulness when it comes to the overall presentation of the finished cake.
- Your organisational abilities.
- Your ability to work in a safe and hygienic manner.

The practical activity has three stages:

- Designing   10 marks
- Implementing   85 marks
- Evaluating   5 marks

SQA will issue a design brief you need to follow:

> ### EXAMPLE
> Design, prepare, bake and finish a cake for a special occasion of your choice.

You will be given a candidate proforma to use to record your work in the practical activity. The person assessing your work will be using general marking principles. These marking instructions indicate how marks should be awarded for each of the skills, techniques and working practices you demonstrate. Marks are allocated in a range of bandings, an example of which is:

- 0 marks if you do not show any evidence of completing the task.
- 1–4 marks if you carry out **some** of the tasks/show **some** evidence.
- 5 marks if you include **all** the required detail/execute techniques to an excellent standard.

STAGE 1: DESIGNING

Stage one has two sections for you to complete: Design Illustration, worth 6 marks, and Plan of Work, worth 4 marks.

DESIGN ILLUSTRATION

This is your opportunity to show exactly what your cake will look like. You can draw it by hand or electronically; it's up to you. You need to show both the top and the side elevations of your cake. You can use the A4 sheet in your proforma to do your illustration or you can use a larger piece of A3 paper and attach it if you would prefer.

To gain the 6 marks available for this section, your illustration needs to include the following information:

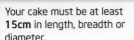

DON'T FORGET

Your cake must be at least **15cm** in length, breadth or diameter.

contd

1   Details of the special occasion that you have decided to make the cake for.

2   The type of cake you have selected. **Your cake must be selected from a light/medium sponge-type cake, a Madeira-type cake, a lightly fruited or heavily fruited cake.**

3   The size of your cake (remember it must be at least 15 cm) and whether it will be round, square or any other shape once finished. Also include information on the size and shape of the cake board/drum you plan to use and whether you will include any decoration on your board.

4   Details of the coating(s) you will use to finish your cake (remember to include all the coatings you plan to use, not just the top coat).

5   Details of the colour scheme you have chosen for both your coating(s) and finishing decorations.

6   Finally, details of any individual finishing decorations you are going to include on your cake.

DON'T FORGET

Your cake board needs to be larger than your cake, plus you need to take account of the extra cm that will be added onto your cake once it is coated in marzipan and sugarpaste or whichever alternative coating you choose.

DON'T FORGET

Don't worry if you aren't a great artist – focus on including all the points of detail you need to be awarded all 6 marks.

> ### EXAMPLE   DESIGN ILLUSTRATION
>
> **Occasion:** The cake is going to be a joint birthday and Christmas cake for my mum as her birthday is on the 23rd of December.
>
> The cake is a 20 cm, round rich fruit cake.
>
> The cake will be coated in apricot jam, natural marzipan and then finished off with a top coat of white royal icing.
>
> The choirboy will have a red body, a white frill around his neck and a peach face, all made out of sugarpaste. He will have piped brown hair made from royal icing. He will be holding a white book made from Mexican paste.
>
> There will be two holly decorations, made from sugarpaste. The veined leaves will be green and the berries red.
>
> Ridged effect in white royal icing.
>
> 26 cm silver drum which has no decoration apart from royal-iced shell border.
>
>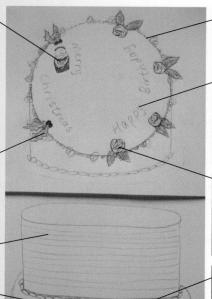
>
> The top edge of the cake will have a piped scroll of white royal icing.
>
> Merry Christmas and Happy Birthday lettering will be cut out from white ½ fondant and ½ flower paste mixture and placed around the top of the cake.
>
> There will be four moulded roses made from red sugarpaste and each will have two rose leaves made from green sugarpaste.
>
> Shell design made from piped white royal icing all around the bottom edge of the cake.

PLAN OF WORK

You have to prepare a Plan of Work for baking and finishing your cake according to your Design Illustration. There are 4 marks available for this section. To gain full marks, you must include the key steps that you will follow at each of the following stages, in the correct sequence:

1   Preparing for both baking and finishing.

2   Planning for baking, cooling and storing your cake.

3   Undertaking the different finishing application techniques you have chosen (remember you must apply **five** finishing application techniques).

4   Undertaking the different finishing decoration techniques you have opted to include on your cake (remember you must apply **five** finishing decoration techniques).

DON'T FORGET

It is important that you take account of hygiene and safety when completing your Plan of Work where appropriate.

PRACTICAL ACTIVITY (CONTINUED)

EXAMPLE

TIMINGS	ACTIVITY	COMMENTS
Session 1 09.00–12.00	Wash hands and put apron on. Prepare tins. Check oven position before preheating to 170°C. Collect, weigh and prepare ingredients. Mix cake to the correct consistency (wash hands after handling raw egg). Deposit into tin*. Bake for 2–3 hours. Clear up. Work on modelling choirboy. Colour sugarpaste red, green and flesh coloured. Check cake. Continue modelling if skewer doesn't come out clear. Remove and cool cake. Clear up. Store cake.	*Remember to include dip on top. Finishing techniques – colouring and modelling.
Session 2 09.00–09.50	Wash hands and put apron on. Prepare cake base (trim and fill). Heat and sieve apricot jam. Spread to coat cake. Knead and roll out marzipan. Smooth and trim. Store cake (**not** in a sealed plastic box). Clear up.	Application techniques – spreading, trimming, coating, rolling, smoothing. Remember to measure to avoid wastage.
Session 3 13.40–14.30	Wash hands and put apron on. Collect cake. Make up royal icing. Coat the cake. Use serrated edge scraper to decorate the sides. Leave to dry. Clear up.	Remember to coat sides before the top. Make sure to cover icing so that **no** air can get in.
Session 4 09.00–12.00	Wash hands and put apron on. Check the consistency of the royal icing. Place cake onto drum. Fill a piping bag and pipe the shell border around base of cake. Pipe scrolls of royal icing around the top edge of the cake. Leave to set. Clear up. Mix ½ sugarpaste and ½ flower paste. Roll out thinly. Lightly rub letter cutter with white fat before cutting out Happy Birthday and Merry Christmas letters. Clear up. Use holly and rose leaf cutters to cut out leaves. Vein leaves. Make four moulded red roses. Secure all decorations onto the cake as per detailed illustration. Store cake carefully. Clear up.	Finishing technique – piping. Finishing technique – use of commercial cutter. Finishing technique – use commercial aid. Finishing technique – modelling.

DON'T FORGET

This is only one example of a Plan of Work. You can decide yourself how you want to do your Plan of Work, as long as you include the key points of information.

DON'T FORGET

Use the information contained within this book as a revision tool. It will remind you how to do some of the techniques, and will help to ensure that you carry out all the required skills and techniques to a high standard.

STAGE 2: IMPLEMENTING

There are 85 marks allocated to this part of the practical activity. The marks are broken down as follows:

SKILL/ACTIVITY	MARKS
Preparing your cake tin(s), weighing, measuring and preparing ingredients	12
Mixing your cake, depositing the mixture in the tin(s), baking, cooling and storing your cake	20
Preparing your cake base for finishing	3
Applying finishing application techniques, using appropriate tools and equipment (you should aim to carry out five techniques, each worth 4 marks)	20
Undertake finishing decoration techniques (you should aim to carry out five techniques, each worth 5 marks)	25
Working safely and hygienically	5

contd

The person assessing you will have an assessment checklist that they will be using to record how you are getting on as you work. Remember, you will be working under controlled conditions, supervised at all times, and all work presented must be your own.

You must choose fillings and coatings that are appropriate for the type of cake you have chosen to make. Fillings/coatings must come from the list below:

FILLING	COATING		
Buttercream	Buttercream	Ganache	Royal icing
Cream	Cream	Melted chocolate	Sugarpaste
Ganache	Frosting	Marzipan/almond paste	
Jam/curds			

DON'T FORGET

It is acceptable for you to carry out some of the finishing application techniques and/or finishing decoration techniques more than once. If you do carry out more than the required five techniques, all techniques will be marked and you will get credit for the ones you do best in.

You must apply **five** finishing application techniques plus **five** finishing decoration techniques to your cake to give yourself the best possible chance of gaining the 45 marks available. The techniques must come from the list below:

FINISHING APPLICATION TECHNIQUE		FINISHING DECORATION TECHNIQUE	
Coating	Smoothing	Colouring	Piping
Piping	Spreading	Crimping	Stencilling
Rolling	Trimming	Embossing	Texturing
		Modelling	Using commercial aids/cutters

You will be required to include two photographs in your proforma. One should be a photograph of your prepared and trimmed and/or filled cake base.

The other should be a photograph of your completed cake.

STAGE 3: EVALUATING

There are 5 marks allocated to evaluating. You need to evaluate your completed cake by commenting on **three** of the following criteria:

- Colour balance
- Design proportion
- Shape
- Texture

Think about the following when completing your evaluation:

- Does my cake meet the brief?
- How does my cake compare to my design illustration?
- What can I say about the overall quality of my finished cake?

When you are asked to evaluate, you cannot just give a statement.

EXAMPLE

Criteria 1: Colour Balance

My cake has three main colours: red, green and white.
✗ *This is a statement, not an evaluative comment.*

Using red and green colours contrast well with the white icing, which I think makes the modelling really stand out.
✔ *This is a point of evaluation.*

Good evaluative words to include in your points include: **which, so, thus, as, therefore.**
Evaluating is all about explaining **why,** not just stating the obvious.

THINGS TO DO AND THINK ABOUT

Before you start your final cake, think very carefully about all the different skills and techniques you have practised throughout your course. This is your opportunity to showcase your talent. Aim to include the techniques that you consider yourself to be most skilful at to ensure you gain maximum marks.

Spend time at the outset researching ideas that meet the brief. Do not over-complicate your design. Think about the time you have been allocated, and ensure that you can complete all finishing decorations to a high standard within that time. Good luck!

SAMPLE RECIPES

RECIPES 1

CONTENTS

BATTENBURG CAKE (SERVES 8)

(approximate cost per recipe = £3.30)

INGREDIENTS

175 g margarine	**Filling and coating**
225 g self-raising flour	2 × 15 ml spoons lemon curd
1 lemon – grated rind and juice	450 g marzipan
175 g caster sugar	Caster sugar for dredging
3 eggs	
few drops pink food colouring	

METHOD

1) Preheat oven to 180°C/Gas mark 4. Grease and line two 450 g loaf tins.

2) Wash the lemon, zest, then squeeze the juice.

3) Cream the margarine and sugar until light and fluffy. Gradually beat in the eggs. Add the lemon juice. Fold in the sieved flour.

4) Divide the mixture into two portions. Add the lemon zest to one portion and pink food colouring to the other. Deposit the mixtures separately into the two prepared tins.

5) Bake for approx 30 minutes – or until a skewer comes out clean. Cool on a wire rack.

6) Trim the edges. Cut each piece of cake in half lengthways, giving four strips.

7) Sandwich alternate colours together with the lemon curd in two layers.

8) Sprinkle some caster sugar onto the work surface and roll the marzipan to a 20 cm × 37 cm oblong. Spread the outside of the cake with lemon curd. Place the cake in the middle of the marzipan. Ease the marzipan around the cake.

9) With the join underneath, pinch the edges and dust with caster sugar before serving.

TOP TIP

If your marzipan has become a little hard, it will become soft and pliable if heated in the microwave for a few seconds on HIGH.

BLACK FOREST GATEAU (SERVES 6)

(approximate cost per recipe = £2.00)

INGREDIENTS

75 g plain flour	50 g chocolate
15 ml spoon cocoa	2.5 ml spoon baking powder
75 g caster sugar	3 eggs
150 ml whipping cream	3 × 15 ml spoons cherry pie filling

METHOD

1) Preheat oven to 220°C/Gas mark 7. Thoroughly grease and line two 15 cm sandwich tins.
2) Sieve flour, baking powder and cocoa into a small mixing bowl.
3) In a large glass bowl, whisk the eggs and caster sugar until the mixture is light and fluffy and leaves a 'ribbon trail' on the surface.
4) Gently fold in the flour mixture with a metal spoon.
5) Divide the mixture equally between the two prepared sponge tins and bake for approximately 10 minutes – until risen and springy to touch.
6) Turn out, remove the paper and cool on a wire tray.
7) Whisk up the cream and spoon into a piping bag fitted with a star nozzle.
8) Gently melt the chocolate. It can either be spread onto greaseproof paper and cut into small triangles when set, or can be placed into a greaseproof piping bag and made into chocolate run-outs. There is also the option of doing a chocolate collar around the outside of the cake (remember a chilled board is needed to be successful here).
9) Sandwich the sponges together with half the cherry pie filling. Spread the remainder on the top of the sponge.
10) Pipe small rosettes of cream around the edge of the cake and decorate with the chocolate triangles/run-outs/chocolate collar.

CARROT CUBES (SERVES 8)

(approximate cost per recipe = £2.90)

INGREDIENTS

2 carrots, grated	2·5 ml cinnamon
2 eggs	200 g cream cheese
200 g self-raising flour	20 g icing sugar
150 g caster sugar	1 g angelica
150 ml oil	50 g fondant icing
50 g walnuts	Orange food colouring

METHOD

1) Preheat oven to 160°C/gas mark 3. Grease and line a 20 cm square tin.
2) Wash and coarsely grate the carrot.
3) Place the oil and sugar in a large bowl. Add the beaten egg and whisk with a balloon whisk.
4) Sieve the flour into the bowl, along with the cinnamon and grated carrot. Chop and add the walnuts. Mix together. Add to the prepared tin.
5) Bake for approximately 30 minutes or until risen, and a skewer comes out clean after being inserted into cake.
6) Remove from oven and leave to cool in the tin for 5–10 minutes, before transferring to a wire rack to cool completely.
7) To make the topping, beat together the cream cheese and icing sugar and spread over the top of the cake. Colour the fondant icing orange and make eight small carrots. Use a small piece of angelica for a leaf.
8) Cut the cake into nine squares and decorate each with a sugarpaste carrot. The cake will keep in an airtight container in a cool place for up to three days.

CHERRY CAKE (SERVES 8)

(approximate cost per recipe = £1.95)

INGREDIENTS

200 g self-raising flour	3 eggs
125 g caster sugar	100 g glacé cherries
125 g margarine	2·5 ml vanilla or almond essence

METHOD

1) Preheat oven to 180°C/Gas mark 4. Grease and line an 18 cm round cake tin (or a 2 lb/900 g loaf tin could be used).
2) Cream the margarine and sugar. Add the beaten eggs with a little of the flour. Add the vanilla or almond essence.
3) Fold in the remaining flour.
4) Wash, half and coat the cherries in a little flour (to prevent them from sinking) and add to the mixture.
5) Place the mixture into the prepared tin. Bake for approximately an hour.
6) The cake is ready when well risen, golden brown on top and a skewer inserted comes out clean.

DON'T FORGET

There is the option to add a mixture of dried glacé fruits instead of just cherries. The addition of some grated lemon/orange zest will add to the flavour.

TOP TIP

The cherries will be very easy to cut up if you use a pair of sharp kitchen scissors that have had their blades dipped in boiling water.

RECIPES 2

DON'T FORGET

If you don't want to use your egg yolks right away, you can freeze them instead. Firstly, you'll need to stabilise the yolks with either a sprinkle of salt for future use in savoury dishes, or a sprinkle of sugar for future use in sweet dishes. By stabilising the yolks, you'll prevent the defrosted yolks from becoming grainy. Add each yolk into a section of an ice cube tray, cover in plastic wrap and freeze.

COCONUT MALLOW JAM SQUARES (SERVES 9)

(approximate cost per recipe = £1.30)

INGREDIENTS

175 g plain flour	25 g desiccated coconut
125 g caster sugar	2 eggs
100 g margarine	4 × 15 ml spoons seedless jam

METHOD

1) Preheat the oven to 180°C/Gas mark 4. Grease and line a 20 cm square tin.
2) Cream the margarine with 50 g of the caster sugar until light and fluffy. Stir in 175 g plain flour until the mixture binds together.
3) Knead lightly on a floured surface then use your fingers to press the mixture evenly into the prepared tin.
4) Fork all over the base and bake for 20 minutes until pale golden. Remove from oven and cool.
5) Spread the jam over the base.
6) Separate the eggs. Whisk the egg whites until stiff then gradually whisk in 75 g caster sugar to make a firm, glossy meringue. Fold in the coconut.
7) Spread the meringue over the jam and sprinkle with 15 ml coconut.
8) Bake for a further 10–15 minutes until the meringue is crisp and browned. Cool, before cutting into nine squares.

CUSTARD CREAMS (SERVES 9)

(approximate cost per recipe = £0.50)

INGREDIENTS

Biscuits	Butter icing
75 g margarine	25 g margarine
100 g self-raising flour	50 g icing sugar
25 g custard powder	Few drops vanilla essence
25 g icing sugar	

METHOD

1) Preheat the oven to 180°C/Gas mark 5. Collect all ingredients. Grease a baking tray.
2) Sieve dry ingredients together onto a plate.
3) Add the margarine into a large bowl. Cream with a wooden spoon. Slowly add the dry ingredients, mixing well after each addition, until a soft dough is formed.
4) Roll into 18 small balls.
5) Place onto the baking tray and flatten with a fork. A cross-cross pattern can be made if wished. Bake for 10–15 minutes, until pale golden brown.
6) Allow to cool on the baking tray before removing to a wire cooling rack.
7) To make the butter icing: soften the margarine in a small bowl and gradually add the sieved icing sugar, mixing thoroughly after each addition.
8) Carefully spread a little butter icing on half of the biscuits, then sandwich the remaining biscuits on top.
9) Dredge lightly with icing sugar.

DUNDEE CAKE (SERVES 8)

[approximate cost per recipe = £2.50]

INGREDIENTS

125 g caster sugar	25 g ground almonds
150 g margarine	10 g whole, blanched almonds
200 g plain flour	75 g sultanas
2·5 ml spoons baking powder	75 g raisins
4 eggs	75 g currants
	25 g mixed peel

METHOD

1) Preheat the oven to 180°C/Gas mark 4. Grease and line an 18 cm deep cake tin.
2) Cream the margarine and sugar together in a large bowl.
3) Sieve the flour and baking powder onto a plate. Add the ground almonds. Beat the eggs.
4) Add beaten egg, alternately with sieved dry ingredients.
5) Mix in the dried fruit (keeping the almonds aside). Put the mixture into the prepared tin. Make a slight dip on the top.
6) Bake for 20 minutes, by which time the slight hollow on top should have levelled out. Arrange the almonds on top.
7) Return to the oven and continue to cook for a further 40–50 minutes.

EASY FRUIT SLICE (SERVES 12)

(approximate cost per recipe = £2.50)

INGREDIENTS

375 g dried mixed fruit	400 g tin condensed milk
150 g self-raising flour	50 g desiccated coconut
5 ml spoon mixed spice	

METHOD

1) Preheat the oven to 160°C/Gas mark 3. Grease and line a 20 cm square/2 lb/900 g loaf tin.

2) Mix all ingredients together and pour into tin.

3) Bake for 40–45 minutes or until skewer comes out clear.

4) Remove and allow to cool before slicing.

EGGLESS FRUIT CAKE (SERVES 8)

(approximate cost per recipe = £1.85)

INGREDIENTS

110 g soft brown sugar	60 ml dry cider
75 g margarine	Zest of 1 lemon
150 ml milk	5 ml spoon ground nutmeg
225 g plain flour	5 ml spoon mixed spice
350 g dried mixed fruit	2·5 ml spoon bicarbonate of soda

METHOD

1) Preheat the oven to 170°C/Gas mark 3. Grease and line an 18 cm/7 in cake tin.

2) Cream the margarine and sugar together until light and fluffy, so that you trap the maximum amount of air. Stir together the milk and bicarbonate of soda then mix all ingredients together in a large bowl. Beat with a wooden spoon until well combined.

3) Deposit mixture into the prepared tin. Dip the back of your hand in milk and use to smooth the surface of the mixture.

4) Bake for two hours until golden brown and firm in the centre.

5) Turn out onto a cooling rack. Leave the lining paper on until cool.

EMPIRE BISCUITS (SERVES 8)

(approximate cost per recipe = £0.65)

INGREDIENTS

100 g margarine	50 g caster sugar
150 g plain flour	100 g icing sugar
15 ml spoon custard powder	2 × 15 ml spoons raspberry jam

METHOD

1) Preheat the oven to 160°C/Gas mark 4. Grease and line a baking tray.

2) Cream the margarine and sugar until light and fluffy.

3) Beat in the sieved flour and custard powder a little at a time to form a stiff dough.

4) Turn the mixture onto a floured surface and roll to 0·5 cm thick.

5) Cut out carefully, using a small or medium sized cutter.

6) Place on greased baking tray and bake for 15–20 minutes, until pale golden brown. Allow to firm slightly before removing onto cooling tray.

7) Sandwich two biscuits together with the jam.

8) Mix the icing sugar with the water to form a thick icing to spread on the top of the biscuits.

9) These biscuits can be decorated using a range of finishing techniques such as piping, stencilling or brush embroidery, or small sugarpaste models can be added.

ALTERNATIVE OPTION

When rolling out the dough, cut out little hearts in half the biscuits using a heart-shaped cutter. These can then be sandwiched together with the jam and dusted lightly on top with icing sugar.

RECIPES 3

GINGER AND TREACLE SPICED TRAYBAKE (SERVES 9)

(approximate cost per recipe = £2.00)

INGREDIENTS

	For the topping
100 g softened butter	
85 g light muscovado sugar	100 g icing sugar
100 g black treacle	2 × 15 ml spoons stem ginger syrup from the jar
150 g self-raising flour	1 finely chopped bulb of stem ginger
1 level tsp (5 ml) baking powder	
2·5 ml spoon ground mixed spice	
2·5 ml spoon ground allspice	
2 eggs	
2 × 15 ml spoons milk	
1 finely chopped bulb of stem ginger from a jar	

METHOD

1) Preheat the oven to 180°C/Gas mark 4. Grease a Swiss roll/baking tray then line with greaseproof paper.
2) Put all the ingredients for the traybake into a large bowl and beat until well blended. Turn the mixture into the prepared tray. Level the top gently with the back of the spatula.
3) Bake in the pre-heated oven for approximately 30 minutes, or until the cake has shrunk from the sides of the tray and springs back when pressed in the centre with your fingertips.
4) Leave to cool in the tray for a few minutes before turning out. Peel off the greaseproof paper and finish cooling on a wire rack.
5) To make the topping, sieve the icing into a bowl and add the ginger syrup and mix until the icing has a smooth spreading consistency. Pour the icing over the cake.
6) Chop the stem ginger and sprinkle on top to decorate. Allow the icing to set before cutting into 8–10 pieces.

ICED LIME TRAYBAKE (SERVES 15)

(approximate cost per recipe = £2.05)

METHOD

1) Preheat the oven to 180°C/Gas mark 4. Lightly grease and line a 20 cm square baking tray.

2) Wash and zest the lime (reserve some for decoration). Squeeze to remove the juice. (Half the juice will be used for the cake, the other half for the icing.)

INGREDIENTS

	For icing
175 g margarine	
175 g golden caster sugar	150 g icing sugar
250 g self-raising flour	½ lime – juice and zest for decoration
5 ml spoon baking powder	
3 eggs	
3 × 15 ml spoons milk	
½ lime – zest and juice	

3) Combine all the cake ingredients in a large bowl and beat well for about 2 minutes or until smooth and thoroughly blended. This can be done with a wooden spoon or an electric whisk.

4) Turn into the prepared tin. Level out the mixture on top. Bake for 35–40 minutes until the cake is well risen, springy to the touch and beginning to shrink away from the sides of the tin.

5) Remove from the oven and leave to cool slightly in the tin before turning out onto a wire cooling rack.

6) To make the icing, sieve the icing sugar into a bowl. Mix in just enough lime juice to give a flowing consistency. Pour over the cooled cake. Decorate with some lime zest before cutting into squares.

LEMON DRIZZLE CAKE (SERVES 8)

(approximate cost per recipe = £1.85)

INGREDIENTS

125 g margarine	**To finish**
2 eggs	50 g granulated sugar
175 g caster sugar	1 lemon – zest and juice
175 g self-raising flour	
1 lemon – zest and juice	

METHOD

1) Preheat the oven to 180°C/Gas mark 4. Grease a 20 cm square cake tin.

2) In a large bowl, cream the margarine and sugar until light and fluffy.

3) Beat the eggs in a cup, before adding to the mixture along with the sieved flour.

4) Finely grate the rind from one of the lemons and stir into the creamed mixture. Squeeze the juice, strain and also add to the creamed mixture. Beat well.

5) Spoon the mixture into the prepared tin. Bake for 25–30 minutes.

6) Using a zester, remove the peel from the remaining lemon. Mix in a small bowl with 25 g of the granulated sugar.

7) Squeeze the lemon. Add the juice to a small saucepan. Add the remaining 25 g of granulated sugar and heat gently in the pan.

8) When the sugar has dissolved, simmer gently for 3–4 minutes, until syrupy.

9) Remove the cake from the oven when ready. With a cocktail stick, prick the cake gently all over.

10) Sprinkle the lemon zest and sugar over the top of the cake. Drizzle over the syrup and leave to cool in the tin.

11) Remove and cut into squares.

MADEIRA CAKE (SERVES 6)

(approximate cost per recipe = £2.00)

INGREDIENTS

175 g margarine	3 eggs
175 g caster sugar	1 lemon
225 g plain flour	7·5 ml spoon baking powder

METHOD

1) Preheat the oven to 160°C/Gas mark 3. The oven shelf needs to be positioned to allow the cake to be one-third up from the bottom. Lightly grease and line a deep 18 cm cake tin (or a 2 lb/900 g loaf tin).

2) Wash the lemon before finely grating the zest. Squeeze the juice.

3) Place all the ingredients into a large bowl and, using an electric whisk, beat for 1 minute, until the mixture is light and fluffy.

4) Place the mixture into the prepared tin and smooth the top. Using a wet tablespoon, make a dip in the centre.

5) Bake for approximately 90 minutes until the cake is golden in colour and a skewer inserted comes out clean.

6) Allow the cake to cool in the tin before removing onto a cooling rack to cool completely.

 TOP TIP

A Madeira cake is protected by its crust. It will last for approximately two weeks, giving one week to decorate and one week to eat. As soon as you start carving it, moisture is lost. One option is to stab with a skewer once removed from the oven and drizzle with cooled sugar syrup. Alternatively, you can cut it and sandwich it with jam/buttercream. This will help retain moisture/keeping qualities.

 DON'T FORGET

To make a **Marbled Cake**, use the basic Madeira Cake recipe except, once the mixture is light and fluffy, separate it out into three bowls. Leave one portion plain. Add a few drops of pink food colouring to the second portion and a few drops of green food colouring to the third portion. Place spoonfuls of the mixture into the tin and carefully smooth the top without mixing.

RECIPES 4

MARBLED CHOCOLATE AND ORANGE LOAF (SERVES 8)

(approximate cost per recipe = £1.90)

INGREDIENTS

125 g caster sugar	50 g plain dark chocolate
125 g margarine	1 orange – zest and 2 × 15 ml spoons of juice
125 g self-raising flour	15 ml spoon cocoa powder
2 eggs	15 ml spoon icing sugar (for dusting)

METHOD

1) Preheat the oven to 180°C/Gas mark 4. Grease and line a 450 g loaf tin.
2) Break up the chocolate and place over a bain-marie and stir gently until melted. Remove and cool slightly.
3) Cream together the margarine and sugar in a large bowl until light and fluffy. Gradually add the beaten eggs.
4) Wash the orange. Zest, then juice the orange. Add the zest and 2 × 15 ml spoons of juice into the bowl.
5) Sieve the flour and gently fold into the mixture. Divide the mixture into two bowls.
6) Add the cocoa powder and melted chocolate into one bowl.
7) Drop tablespoonfuls of each cake mixture into the prepared tin – alternating between the orange and chocolate mixtures. Swirl the mixtures together to give a marbled effect.
8) Bake in the preheated oven for 40 minutes, or until a skewer inserted comes out clean.
9) Remove from the oven. Leave in the tin for 5 minutes before removing onto a cooling rack.
10) Before serving, dust the top of the cake with icing sugar.

MINCEMEAT TEA LOAF (SERVES 12)

(approximate cost per recipe = £2.40)

INGREDIENTS

225 g self-raising flour	250 g mincemeat
125 g margarine	25 g glacé cherries
2 eggs	2·5 ml spoon mixed spice
75 g soft brown sugar	75 g flaked almonds
5 ml spoon lemon juice	10 ml spoon milk

Method

1) Preheat the oven to 180°C/gas mark 4. Grease and line a 2 lb/900 g loaf tin.
2) Sieve the flour and mixed spice into a large bowl. Add the margarine and rub in until the mixture resembles fine breadcrumbs.
3) Set aside 2 tablespoons of the flaked almonds. Add the remaining almonds to the bowl, along with the sugar and glacé cherries.
4) Make a well in the centre and add the eggs, mincemeat, lemon juice and milk. Gently fold together.
5) Spoon into the prepared loaf tin. Smooth the top before sprinkling the reserved almonds on top.
6) Bake for 30 minutes. Check. The loaf may need to be covered with foil to protect almonds from burning. Bake for a further 30 minutes, or until skewer comes out clean.
7) Remove and leave in tin to cool for 10 minutes.

POUND CAKE (SERVES 8)

(approximate cost per recipe = £1.65)

Pound Cake was traditionally a way of remembering the weight of the ingredients without the need to remember a recipe. It was also referred to as 1234 cake in America. It can be adapted in many ways by the addition of different flavourings such as lemon, coconut, pecans, blueberries.

INGREDIENTS

125 g self-raising flour	2 eggs
125 g caster sugar	10 ml vanilla essence
125 g butter	

METHOD

1) Preheat the oven to 190°C/Gas mark 5. Grease and line a 450 g loaf tin or 15 cm round cake tin.
2) Cream the butter and sugar together until light and fluffy.
3) Using an electric whisk, add the egg, flour and vanilla essence and whisk until all ingredients are mixed through.
4) Spoon the mixture into the prepared tin and bake for approximately 45 minutes.
5) When a skewer inserted comes out clean, remove from the oven. The cake can then be decorated in a variety of ways.

RICH FRUIT CAKE (SERVES 8)

(approximate cost per recipe = £4.15)

INGREDIENTS

250 g plain flour	25 g flaked almonds
200 g soft brown sugar	50 g glacé cherries
200 g margarine	5 ml spoon mixed spice
4 eggs	500 g mixed dried fruit
15 ml spoon treacle	2·5 ml spoon nutmeg
25 g ground almonds	

TOP TIP

Once the mixture has been deposited into the tin, and a dip has been made in the centre, run your fist under the tap and sprinkle the water on your hand over the top of the cake. Cover the cake tin with a baking tray as you put it into the oven. This will serve to add additional moisture when your cake is baking and should help you to achieve a perfectly flat top to your cake when it comes out of the oven... just what you need when it comes to decorating it.

METHOD

1) Preheat the oven to 170°C/Gas mark 3. The oven shelves may need to be adjusted so that the cake sits one third up from the bottom of the oven. Thoroughly grease and line a deep 15–18 cm cake tin.

2) Prepare the fruit and mix in the chopped nuts and treacle.

3) Sieve the dry ingredients onto a plate.

4) Wash and cut the cherries into quarters and add to the dry ingredients.

5) Cream together the margarine and brown sugar. Add the beaten egg alternately with the sieved dry ingredients and mix well.

6) Stir in the dried fruit mixture.

7) Deposit the mixture into the prepared tin. Smooth over the surface with a palette knife before using a wet metal spoon to make a well in the centre. Bake for 2–3 hours.

8) The cake is cooked when it is well risen and brown in colour. A skewer should come out clean when inserted.

9) Remove and cool. A few spoonfuls of alcohol such as brandy or sherry can be drizzled over the cake at the cooling stage to add flavour.

SPONGE DROPS (SERVES 10)

(approximate cost per recipe = £1.30)

INGREDIENTS

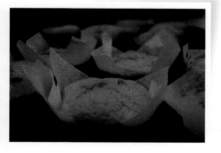

50 g caster sugar	2 × 15 ml spoons jam
50 g self-raising flour	150 g whipping cream
2 eggs	5 ml spoon icing sugar for dusting

METHOD

1) Preheat the oven to 200°C/Gas mark 6. Lightly grease two baking trays.

2) Whisk the eggs and sugar together until the mixture is thick and creamy and 'ribbon trail' is achieved.

3) Gently fold in the sieved flour. This could be done over a bain-marie.

4) Place small spoonfuls of mixture, well apart, on the baking trays and bake for approximately 5 minutes.

5) Carefully remove and cool on a wire rack.

6) Whisk the cream. When the sponges are cold, sandwich two together with some jam and cream. Dust with icing sugar to serve.

RECIPES 5

SULTANA CAKE (SERVES 8)

(approximate cost per recipe = £2.25)

INGREDIENTS

175 g plain flour	2 eggs
100 g caster sugar	5 ml spoon baking powder
200 g sultanas	Grated rind of ½ lemon
175 g margarine	

METHOD

1) Preheat the oven to 170°C/Gas mark 3. Adjust the oven shelf to allow the cake to sit one-third up from the bottom of the oven. Grease and line a 15–18 cm round cake tin.

2) Wash the lemon and finely grate the rind.

3) Beat the eggs in a small bowl. Sieve the flour and baking powder onto a plate.

4) Cream the margarine and sugar together until light and fluffy. Add the beaten egg alternately with the sieved dry ingredients to give a dropping consistency.

5) Add the fruit and lemon rind and mix well.

6) Deposit the mixture into the prepared tin and bake for approximately 90 minutes. The cake is ready when lightly browned in colour and a skewer inserted comes out clean.

7) Allow the cake to cool in the tin before removing onto a cooling rack.

SWISS ROLL (SERVES 6)

(approximate cost per recipe = £0.85)

Ingredients

50 g self-raising flour	2 eggs
50 g caster sugar	2 × 15 ml spoons jam

METHOD

1) Preheat the oven to 220°C/Gas mark 7. Lightly grease and line a Swiss roll tin.

2) Whisk the eggs and sugar together until the mixture is light in colour, thick and creamy and 'ribbon trail' is achieved.

3) Add the sieved flour and, using a metal spoon (or balloon whisk), gently fold in the flour.

4) Carefully pour the mixture into the prepared tin. Gently move the mixture around in the tin until it is level and into the corners.

5) Bake the sponge for 8–10 minutes. When the sponge is cooked it should be well risen, set and golden in colour.

6) Lightly dredge a piece of greaseproof paper, slightly bigger than the baking tray, with caster sugar.

7) Place the jam in a bowl and stir it thoroughly so that it will spread easily.

8) Remove the Swiss roll from the oven and working quickly, turn it out onto the sugared paper. Remove the lining paper. Trim away the edges of the sponge with a sharp knife.

9) Spread the jam quickly over the sponge.

10) Working from the narrow end, gently fold the first part of the roll with the fingers, then continue the rolling by pulling the paper away from you over the sponge.

11) Place the Swiss roll on a wire tray with the rounded edge uppermost so that it is allowed to cool.

DON'T FORGET

The basic Swiss roll recipe can be adapted in a variety of ways – for example, by adding in cocoa for a chocolate version. Make a **St Clements Roll** by adding the grated rind of an orange to the eggs and sugar and use lemon curd instead of jam to roll up. A **Raspberry Meringue Roll** can be made by rolling up the Swiss roll sponge with greaseproof paper instead of jam. Once cooled, it can be unrolled and filled with cream and raspberries.

VICTORIA SANDWICH (SERVES 6)

(approximate cost of recipe = £1.65)

INGREDIENTS

150 g margarine	2 × 15 ml spoons jam
150 g caster sugar	15 ml spoon icing sugar
150 g self-raising flour	
3 eggs	

METHOD

1) Preheat the oven to 170°C/Gas mark 4. Lightly grease and line the base of two 15 cm sponge tins.

2) Cream the margarine and the sugar until soft, light and creamy in texture.

3) Beat the eggs in a small bowl. Sieve the flour onto a plate.

4) Add the eggs a little at a time along with a little of the sieved flour beating the mixture continually until all the egg is used.

5) Gently fold in the remaining flour. The mixture should be a 'dropping consistency' which falls easily from a wooden spoon. A little water may be added at this stage if necessary.

6) Divide the mixture evenly between the two sponge tins and place in the oven to bake for approximately 20 minutes. The sponges should be well risen, golden brown in colour and bounce back when pressed.

7) Leave the sponges to cool for a few minutes before gently removing the sponges from the tins and placing them on a wire tray to become completely cold.

8) Sandwich the sponges together with the jam, and dust the top with some icing sugar.

DON'T FORGET

A variety of flavourings can be added to the sponge mixture – for example, orange, lemon or lime – add the finely grated rind of the fruit along with a 15 ml spoon of the fruit juice to the creamed mixture before adding the flour.

Cocoa can be added to give a chocolate version. Dissolve 10 ml of instant coffee in 15 ml boiling water and add to the sponge, and sandwich the cake with chocolate spread to make a **Mocha Sandwich Cake**.

Cinnamon can be added to the sponge, and the jam can be replaced by stewed apple for a **Cinnamon & Apple Sandwich Cake**.

Add the grated rind of an orange to the cake and sandwich with orange marmalade for an **Orange Sandwich Cake**.

VIENNESE FINGERS (SERVES 8)

(approximate cost of recipe = £0.60)

INGREDIENTS

125 g margarine	50 g icing sugar
125 g plain flour	25 g margarine
25 g icing sugar	50 g chocolate

METHOD

1) Preheat the oven to 180°C/Gas mark 4. Grease a baking tray.

2) Cream together the margarine and sugar in a large bowl.

3) Gradually add the sieved flour.

4) Place the mixture into a piping bag containing a large star nozzle.

5) Pipe an even number of fingers. Bake for 8–10 minutes.

6) Remove and leave to cool on a cooling rack.

7) Cream together the margarine and icing sugar to make the butter icing. Sandwich two fingers together.

8) Melt the chocolate and dip the ends of the biscuits in the chocolate.

DON'T FORGET

The same recipe can be used to pipe star-shaped biscuits, which can then be sandwiched together with cream and jam.

GLOSSARY

Additives
Substances that are added to food to give different qualities such as preservatives or colourings.

Aeration
Process by which air is added – for example, whisking egg whites traps air bubbles.

Artista soft
A non-toxic, non-edible air drying modelling paste.

Bain-marie
A water bath. May be used to gently melt chocolate.

Ball tool
Used to make indentations, such as eye sockets, in a sugarpaste model.

Bas-Relief
A technique to produce built-up sugarpaste shapes/models.

Blossom cutter
Used to make small filler flowers. Often part of a set of three plunger cutters.

Brush embroidery
A decorative technique whereby a piped royal icing outline is brushed inwards while still soft.

Calyx
Part of a sugar flower where the petals join the stem.

Caramelisation
When sugar is heated, it melts and a caramel is formed.

Coagulation
On the application of heat, proteins change. They first denature and then set – for example, when cooking an egg the white changes from opaque to white. Once protein has coagulated, the changes are irreversible.

Cold porcelain
A non-edible modelling paste made from cornflour, glue and baby oil.

Collagen
Collagen is a protein found in meat.

Conduction
When heat passes from one hot area to another – for example, heating a pan on the hob.

Convection
Heat transfers through liquid or gases in a current – for example, in an oven.

Crimper
A tool used to pinch together edges of soft icing to give a decorative effect.

Crystallisation
When sugar and water are boiled, the water is driven off and a thick syrup is formed. This sets on cooling – that is, it reverts back to its crystal form.

Denaturation
Denaturation is a process where proteins lose their structure when heated.

Density
A measure of how compact particles or molecules are in a liquid or solid.

Dextrinization
When starch is subjected to dry heat, a chemical change takes place. The starch molecules break down into dextrin. Dextrins are starch chains made up of glucose molecules.

Dowel
Either wooden or plastic, these are sticks that are used to support cake layers.

Dresden tool
Has a sharp or veining end used for scoring sugarpaste and a blunt end used for scoring. Also useful for frilling edges.

Edible glue
Also known as sugar glue. Used to stick together dried pieces of icing.

Embossing
A decorative technique whereby a design is pressed into soft sugarpaste using a special embossing tool or everyday objects such as buttons.

Emulsification
Emulsification is the property that allows fats and oils to mix with water, preventing them from separating out. Lecithin found in egg yolk is a natural emulsifier.

Fermentation
The process of using yeast to convert sugar to carbon dioxide and alcohol. Used to make bread.

Filigree
Ornamental fine lacework that can be piped directly onto a cake or piped onto paper and removed and placed onto a cake when dry. Also called Cornelli.

Firm Peak
Used to describe royal icing once it has been beaten. It will stand firmly and hold its shape.

Flower paste
A paste that can be rolled thinly to create hand-modelled items, such as flowers, that need to set firm.

Foam
As eggs are whisked, air bubbles are beaten into the liquid and the protein in egg denatures. These denatured protein strands make the mixture more stable. Egg white alone can trap as much as seven times its own volume in air. This is called a foam.

Fondant icing
Another name for sugarpaste.

Fortification
The addition of vitamins and minerals into foods to increase their nutritional value or replace nutrients lost during processing.

Ganache
Ganache is a glaze, icing, sauce, or filling for pastries made from chocolate and cream.

Garret frill
A frill made from flower paste that is used to decorate around the sides or edge of a cake.

Gelatinisation
On the application of heat, starch grains absorb water, swell and burst, forming a gel.

Glace
A French term meaning 'glossy'. Glace icing is made using icing sugar and warm water.

Glazing
A shiny brown top to a product like a scone can be achieved if beaten egg is brushed on top before cooking.

Gluten
The protein found in flour.

Gum tragacanth
A powder that can be added to sugarpaste to stiffen it.

Hydrogenation
The process of artificially hardening a liquid oil to a solid fat by the addition of extra hydrogen.

Lipids
Lipids are small molecules. Fats are lipids that are solid at room temperature. Oils are lipids that are liquid at room temperature.

Maillard browning
Maillard browning is a chemical reaction that occurs between amino acids and sugar, usually resulting in a change of colour to dark brown.

Marbling
A technique whereby two colours of sugarpaste are partially blended to create streaks. Important not to over-knead.

Mexican paste
A strong paste used for modelling. Sets firm.

Nozzle
Another name for a piping tube. They come in lots of different shapes and sizes to allow you to create different effects.

Overpiping
When a second line of piping is piped on top of the exisiting line. Often used when doing writing to make the outline stand out.

Pastillage
A firm paste used for making flowers and models. It sets firm when dry.

Posy pick
Inserted into the top of a cake and used to hold wires.

Radiation
Transfer of heat in rays onto the surface of another object – for example, grilling bread to make toast.

Ribbon insertion
Ribbon or paste strips inserted into a cake to look as if the ribbon has been threaded through the icing.

Ribbon trail
Test for readiness in a whisked sponge, where mixture should stay on the surface for 30 seconds without sinking in.

Royal icing
A mixture of icing sugar and egg white which hardens when it dries.

Shortening
Refers to how 'short' or crumbly the texture of a product is.

Smoother
A flat plastic tool that you rub over the top and sides of a cake to give a smooth surface.

Snail trail
A piping technique where a trail of small teardrops touch each other. Often used around the base of a cake.

Soft peak
Term used to describe royal icing that stands in peaks but droops over at the tip.

Stamen
The central part of a flower. They come in a wide variety of colours and sizes.

Stencil
Used to add a design to a cake by masking off areas with a template of a shape or pattern you do not want coloured.

Stippling
A method of adding colour onto a cake by using a brush.

Sugarpaste
Soft icing paste that can be used to coat cakes or produce models. Also known as fondant icing.

SugarVeil
A decorative icing that can be cut or shaped when set.

Texturing
Adding texture to the surface – for example, using a scouring pad, grater, brush or texturing pad.

Veiner
Used in the production of leaves, soft paste is pressed into a veiner to leave an impression of veins.

Viscosity
A measure of how easily a liquid flows.